The Brass Candlesticks

Irene Levy

authorHOUSE®

AuthorHouse™
1663 Liberty Drive
Bloomington, IN 47403
www.authorhouse.com
Phone: 1 (800) 839-8640

This book is a work of non-fiction. Unless otherwise noted, the author and the publisher make no explicit guarantees as to the accuracy of the information contained in this book and in some cases, names of people and places have been altered to protect their privacy.

Published by AuthorHouse 12/14/2015

ISBN: 978-1-5049-6254-4 (sc)
ISBN: 978-1-5049-6253-7 (e)

Print information available on the last page.

This book is printed on acid-free paper.

Thank you to the following people, without whom the publication of this book would not have been possible:

Charles Rubin
Richard Ehrlich
Douglas Hayes
Janet Elin
Mariel Falk - Front Cover Designer
Barton Midwood - Editor

In memory of my brother, Louis Rubin,
and his wife, Ruth Rubin

PREFACE

I have always wanted to write a book about our family; although our family's story is far from unique, it's still our story. I want to leave a history for my children, grandchildren, and future generations. Over the years I have listened to many people, young and old, say, "I wish I had asked my parents and grandparents what life was like when they were kids." Some people never take the time to learn the real roots of their family, or what it was like to grow up in a country that did not want you. Whether your roots are Russian or Polish, Italian or African, Asian or Irish, whether your family's religion is Jewish, Catholic, Muslim, Hindu, or Buddhist, the histories are very similar. Jews were once slaves in Egypt as the Africans were slaves in the United States. Hate, persecution, slavery, famine: every group has suffered its own indignities.

It is important to know who you are; it helps to make you a whole person. Jewish children learn parts of the Torah for their Bat or Bar Mitzvah. This is to preserve the Jewish religious history, one person at a time. The hope is that if all the Torahs of the world were destroyed, there would be enough people left to put it all back together again,

My hope is that this book will answer many questions that future generations may have. In any case, if one person reads it and is inspired to add to it, my effort will not have been in vain.

The inspiration for writing this story came to me on a Friday night while I was visiting my daughter Linda and her family. We all stood and watched her light the Shabbat candles in the brass candlesticks which once belonged to my great grandmother and grandmother and which one day will belong to my granddaughters. The candlesticks have been in our family for over a hundred years. They made the long voyage from Russia to America with my grandmother; like her, they crossed the Atlantic Ocean and were among the few precious belongings my grandmother brought with her to the new world. I do not know who used them first or who will be last to use them, but I hope they will continue to hold Shabbat candles for many generations to come.

As I stood there watching Linda, my mind started to wander. I began to think about what I knew of the history of the Jews who lived in Eastern Europe in the 19th century. The first modern pogrom against Jews is considered to be the anti-Jewish riots that occurred in 1821 in Odessa, where, it was reported, fourteen Jews were killed following the death of the Greek Orthodox patriarch in Istanbul. Other commentators consider the first pogrom to have been the 1859 riots against the Jews, which also took place in Odessa. The term "pogrom" became commonly used after the wave of anti-Jewish riots that swept through south-western Imperial Russia from 1881 to 1884, following the assassination of Czar Alexander II on March 13, 1881. It was believed that the

Jews were responsible for the assassination, in particular a Jewish woman named Gesya Gelfman. In fact, her only crime was being born into a Jewish home and being a "close associate" of the assassins. The assassins were actually atheists but rumors spread by the press inspired "retaliatory" attacks by Christians on Jewish communities. During April of 1881, thousands of Jewish homes were destroyed, many families were thrown into poverty and large numbers of men, women and children were injured or killed in over one hundred sixty towns throughout the Russian Empire. These pogroms intensified and became more hideous as time went on, forcing the emigration of many Jews to America and elsewhere. Another wave of pogroms took place from 1903 to 1906, leaving over two thousand Jews dead and many more injured and homeless.

HARRY'S FAMILY

Our story begins, in 1893 in Zhitomir, a small Russian village outside of Kiev. It was a time of great unrest in Eastern Europe. It was the month of April and Cantor Leib Rabinowitz was once again late for work. It was just a little over a year since his beautiful wife Sarah had died in childbirth. She was only twenty-five, and it was to be her fourth child. Sadly, Leib had lost them both, but he still had three young children at home to take care of. It was hard being both a mother and father to his children. Sarah had been the one who ran the household, cared for the children, and took care of all of her husband's needs.

Leib and Sarah had been married for seven wonderful years, but four pregnancies in seven years was just too much for her frail body to handle. As was the tradition in Europe at that time, theirs was an arranged marriage set up by a matchmaker *(Shad Chan in Hebrew)*. Both Leib and Sarah were children of Rabbis. Sarah was sixteen years old when she married Leib. They had never met but fell in love soon after they married. Young girls from poor families were often married to older men who had lost their wives and needed someone to care for their children and home.

Leib's family and neighbors tried to help him as much as they could. It was important for him to continue working and not lose his job. Leib's children, Leah 6, Dora 5, and Morris 2, were too young to understand what had happened to their mother. All they knew was that she was no longer around and uncles, aunts, cousins, or neighbors were with them while their father was at work. As the Cantor of the Carpenters Synagogue in Zhitomir, Leib had a very busy life. In his position, he was considered a very important man in his community. The members of the congregation were very happy with their Cantor, because he had a kind heart and a deep rich singing voice. He was also very handsome and had blue eyes, and light brown hair. Leib was slim and stood about 5'5" tall, which was a good height for a man in those days.

Rabbi Yankel Weinman was the Chief Rabbi at the Carpenters' Synagogue, where Leib was the Cantor. One day the Rabbi saw Leib in the hall and asked him to join him in the study. On the way in Leib began to worry. He thought, "What could the Rabbi want from me? Have I done anything wrong? Am I going to be fired?" Things were not going well for Jews anywhere in Russia; everyone was having a hard time, and Zhitomir was no different. By the time he got into the Rabbi's study Leib had worked himself into a state of panic.

As Leib entered the room Rabbi Weinman said: "Sit down, my son, I have been asked to speak to you on behalf of the elders. They want me to let you go, because it has always been our practice here to have only married Cantors lead our congregation. It has been a year since Sarah of blessed memory passed away. Your year of mourning year is over, and I am truly sorry that I can no longer protect you. But if you will hear me out I have an idea that will help us both."

At this point Leib saw that the Rabbi was getting just as nervous as he was. Leib thought, "What could be so hard for the Rabbi to speak to me about that he appears to be nervous?" The Rabbi cleared his throat and began to speak; "I would really like to help you and your family and maybe help my own daughter at the same time. As you know my daughter, Fanny, is not yet married. Her betrothed was killed three years ago while serving in the Tsar's Army. She has not been able to move on and I think if you got to know each other maybe you could both find some happiness together." The Rabbi told Leib, "I am not pushing; I am only suggesting. Just promise me you will think about it. I will try to hold the elders off as long as I can before they start to look for a new Cantor." Leib took a deep breath and said; "Thank you Rabbi, for trying to help me and my family. I will think about it."

Then Leib got up, shook the Rabbi's hand, and left the room as fast as he could. After Leib was out in the hallway, he whispered to himself "No pressure indeed." After Leib was further away, he thought, "I love my job and my children need a mother. It would be so hard to find another job as a Cantor as more and more synagogues are being burned down or just abandoned. People everywhere are fleeing for their lives. I need to keep this job as long as possible." Leib began to think about the Rabbi's daughter Fanny. His first thought was that she was pretty, sweet, shy, very kind, helpful, but she always seemed a little sad. Leib knew she had lost her true love and he of all people could understand how she felt. Leib decided he would have to give this a little more thought. He had never thought of Fanny as a possible wife and mother for his children. But the more he considered it, the more he was convinced the Rabbi's idea might not be so bad.

The next day was a Monday, and Leib took a walk into town and headed toward the little bake shop where he knew Fanny worked. He had been going into the shop every Friday since Sarah had died, to pick up the challah for Shabbat, as well as a sweet treat for the children when he could.

Leib stood outside for a short time just looking in the window and watched her work, and he noticed that she was very nice to the customers, always greeting them by name. This was easy since most of them were members of her father's congregation. Leib also noticed that Fanny was dressed for work, plain, neat, and clean, just as she dressed when she attended Sabbath services at the Temple. After about a half hour, Leib got up the courage to walk into the bakery.

Fanny saw him come in. "Hello, Cantor Rabinowitz. How are you doing today?" Leib answered, "Fine, thank you and I hope you are doing well also." "Yes, I am, and thank you for asking. What brings you into the shop today? I never see you in here unless it's Friday." As Fanny was speaking to Leib, she was thinking what a nice man he was. This was the longest conversation she had ever had with the Cantor and she found that he was very easy to talk to. Fanny had always liked the Cantor, and felt he was doing a wonderful job caring for his children on his own.

Leib asked her how she liked working in the bakery. She told him she loved working in the bakery, because at the end of the day she could take home some of the bread that had not been sold that day. "We give the rest to the families that are in need here in the neighborhood," she said. Then, before she knew what she was saying, she asked Leib; "Would you and your children like to join us for Sabbath dinner this Friday night?" Leib answered, "Yes, we would be honored."

Fanny had thought she could never enjoy the company of another man. She and Jake had set their wedding date and then he was told he had to join the army. He was to leave in a few weeks' time and Fanny had wanted to move up the date of the marriage, but Jake wanted to wait "just in case something happens to me." Three months later Jake was killed. She had felt as though she would never be whole again. But now, perhaps, it was time for her to move on.

After Leib left Fanny at her father's house, he began walking home. Out of nowhere, a sudden cold wind blew up. Leib had to duck to avoid being hit by a flying tin can; it brought to mind just how harsh his life was and that things could change in an instant. Just like the tin can being tossed by the wind, he understood you never knew when something would come along and change your life forever.

At Shabbat dinner the following Friday night Fanny was delightful. The dinner she cooked was a feast like he had not had since Sarah died. As the woman of the house, she lit the Sabbath candles in the brass candlesticks that had belonged to her grandmother and mother, and had been passed on to her. Fanny wore a lovely dress and for the first time since Jake died, seemed to be very happy. After they finished the meal, Fanny played with the children. She read them stories and sang songs and they were content and sleepy by the time they left. The smile on her father's face reflected the feeling in his heart that he had been right. These two young people could help each other heal and maybe learn to love and he would yet live to be a grandfather.

Within a month's time, Fanny and Leib were to be married. Finally the day arrived. Since Fanny was the Rabbi's daughter, the whole town was invited to the wedding, which took place outdoors on a beautiful bright Friday night at midnight, under heaven above with a sky full of twinkling stars, and beautiful moonlight. Fanny wore her mother's wedding dress.

The wedding between Leib and Fanny was a traditional Orthodox Jewish wedding. The custom for this wedding is outlined in Genesis 22, verse 17. The verse gives God's assurance to Abraham "That in blessing I will multiply your seed as the stars of the heaven, and as the sand which is on the seashore; and your seed shall possess the gate of your enemies." At the beginning of the wedding ceremony, the groom stands under a canopy awaiting his bride. The bride then walks up the center isle with her parents. The groom then is seated. The bride then circles around the groom seven times. This circling of the groom has a great holy significance. The first significance is that there are seven days in a week, and the Sabbath is on the seventh day. The seven circles around the groom are to protect the groom from evil spirits and demons. The evil spirits seek to deny the newly married couple the fulfillment they seek from their marriage. The circle is a shape that evil spirits and demons cannot penetrate and is a shape without beginning or end. Finally, in a Jewish home, the man is as a King, and a King is always encircled by his soldiers that protect him. In the next step of the wedding, the bride will stand on the groom's right side and both will recite their vows to each other. After the vows are finished, the groom places the wedding ring on the bride's right index finger, in order to show the ring to the wedding guests. Later, after the ceremony, the bride will move the wedding ring to the fourth finger of her left hand.

After the wedding celebration was over and all the guests had left, Fanny's father arranged for a family from his Temple congregation to take care of the children so the newly-weds could have at least one blissful, quiet night together. The next morning Fanny moved into her new home right away. After the children returned from the neighbors, she got them dressed and fed them their breakfast.

On the first Friday night in her new home, and with her father and husband at the table, Fanny lit the Sabbath candles in brass candlestick holders. She recited the ancient prayer to welcome in the *"Sabbath Bride"* and then added her own small prayer. She thanked God for her good fortune in having found a man who loved her and was willing to give her a home and entrust to her the care of his children.

Fanny worked very hard to keep their home in order. She also helped the children learn to read Hebrew and sang the same songs to them that her mother had sung to her. Every Friday night she prepared a Sabbath dinner for Lieb and the children. Neither Fanny nor her father ever thought of the children as being Leib's, they both thought of the children as theirs. They loved each of them very much and they in turn loved them back.

One day Leib's oldest child, Leah, asked Fanny why she had waited so long to get married. Leah knew that by the time most girls turned twenty-two they had at least one or two children. Fanny sat down and pulled Leah onto her lap. She then started to explain the story to her. "Well, sweetheart, when I was eighteen, I was supposed to marry my first true love, Jake. He was handsome, brave, and strong, and we had been friends since we were children. I always thought he would be my husband one day. Then he was taken into the army and we promised to marry when he returned. He was in the war for only three months when he died saving a friend's life. It made me very angry and very sad; because I thought I would never love or marry someone again. Then Fate, and my father, played a hand in my future. Your father was also hurt and very sad after your mother died. It just seemed we had so much in common and so much to give each other that we got married and then fell in love. Now I've got a wonderful husband and three beautiful children, and I could not love you more if I had given birth to all of you myself. In this day and age we must be very grateful for any happiness we can have." Leah replied, with the innocence of a child. "I'm sorry that your friend Jake died, but I am happy for us. We have you as a new Mama, and now Papa is not sad anymore." Leah kissed Fanny's cheek, hopped off her lap and ran outside to play.

A few months after they married Fanny realized she was pregnant with her first child. She could not be happier. Not only had God blessed her with a wonderful family but now a child of her very own. The children were very happy that they would have a new baby to play with. Morris jumped up and down when he heard the news. "I hope it's a baby brother, I want a baby brother." "Why?" Papa asked. "Well, I already have two sisters and now I won't be the only boy any more. Now I will be a big brother and boss my little brother around." Everyone laughed.

The following nine months seemed to fly by before anyone realized it was almost time for the baby to be born, and Leib began to worry, and he would pray daily; and ask God not to take another wife and child from him.

As Fanny's pregnancy progressed the children were as helpful as young children could be. They all made as little noise as possible, helped Fanny carry the wash, do the dishes and whatever else Mama and Papa asked of them. On March 4th, 1896 the Rabinowitz family welcomed a new son. He was named Heshel after Leib's father, who had passed away two years earlier. Leib knew his son would be blessed as he had not one but two grandfathers who were learned Rabbis. Little did Leib know what was in store for him with this blessed son of his.

HARRY

Heshel was a beautiful child with blond hair and bright blue eyes. Leib wished his father had been alive to see the birth of his new grandson. Leib would often think of his father and about how important he had been to the family and his congregation. Rabbi Heshel Rabinowitz was always sought out when there was a need for wisdom and fairness. He was revered and idolized by Jews for hundreds of miles around. Some traveled for days just to listen to him speak in the Synagogue and receive his counsel. With his family growing larger, Leib began to miss him more than ever. When Heshel was eight days old, the ceremony of Berit Milah (circumcision) was carried out by Fanny's father, and it was a very happy and proud time for the whole family.

As a baby and young child Heshel was well taken care of by all of his family. Everyone spoiled him and as he grew older they admired his free spirit. As the years passed, more children were added to the Rabinowitz family. With each birth, Leib worried that it might take his wonderful wife from him. But Fanny was much stronger than Sarah had been and the births were easier for her.

In 1898, two years after the birth of Heshel, Yankel was born. He was named for Fanny's father who died only a few months earlier. Then two years later came the darling of the family, Ida. Heshel loved Ida very much and she was everyone's favorite sister. Last but surely not least, seven years after Heshel, Albert was born. In Leib's household, there was never any mention of half brothers and half sisters. They were all the same, just one big happy family.

Heshel was a very smart child, but unlike the rest of the children, he did not take his religious studies very seriously. He was a dreamer and daredevil, very aware of what was going on around him. He loved to take his baby sister Ida out into the fields and show her flowers, birds, and trees. He had no desire to be cooped up all day learning Torah. He felt there was too much to see and explore. Heshel thought he needed to learn about how to live in the forest and survive off the land. He always asked questions of farmers and hunters. He knew at an early age that the family would someday have to flee. He needed to be able to survive and save his family. For some strange reason he just felt this task would fall to him.

As each year passed, it was getting harder and harder to be a Jew in Russia. With the little money Leib was able to earn he managed to feed and clothe his family, and the older children helped where they could to help their father. They collected eggs, searched for fire wood, and helped neighbors with whatever was needed.

Many of the young healthy men eighteen years of age or older were being taken into the Army to fight. Heshel had always known he was not going to fight in any war, especially not for something he did not believe in. He knew he would run away before he was of age to be taken away and forced to serve.

As Heshel approached manhood, he kept reminding his family that one day he would go to America, and become a rich man and move them all away from this harsh life in Russia. It may have been the only home he had ever known, but he also knew it had to be better someplace else. Leib was really afraid for his family. In the spring of 1904, Leib's oldest daughter Leah, met and married a man named Isaac Modell. Her father married them in the Carpenters' Synagogue. In 1905 Isaac took Leah to America, and they settled in a place called Brooklyn, New York. Soon after their arrival in America letters were sent to the family in Russia. The letters that got through begged the rest of the family to follow, even though everyone knew it was not easy and would take a great deal of money for the whole family to get to America.

In March 1911, Heshel turned fifteen and he considered himself a man. and wanted to do all he could to help his family. It was Spring and Fanny was getting ready for Passover, the holiday that celebrates the flight of the Jewish people out of slavery in Egypt to freedom. Making the Passover Seder would be hard this year because food was very scarce. Fanny was determined to do the best she could, because nobody knew what the next year would bring. When the family gathered around the table and waited for the candles to be lit and prayers to be said, Heshel looked out the window. He noticed a homeless man sitting alone on a bench. How alone he looked. Heshel knew enough about Torah and the laws of Passover to know that you were supposed to take in the hungry. (*"Let all who are hungry enter and be fed."*) Heshel also knew that there was hardly enough on the table to feed his family, let alone strangers. The sight of this man bothered Heshel more than even he could understand. Heshel had eaten that morning and the day before but he could not even guess when the poor man he was watching had last eaten. Without saying a word, Heshel left the table and went outside and brought the poor man in and gave up his seat and his food. His family said nothing, but the pride in their faces said it all. Study was not everything; it was what was in your heart that counted the most. Doing a Mitzvot, *(a good deed,)* helping the less fortunate is what our religion is all about. On this very important night, Heshel proved beyond a doubt that he had a good heart and knew what it meant to be a Jew. This would not be his first Mitzvot or his last, but this one meant the most to his father and the rest of the family witnessed it.

The pogroms were getting closer and closer each day, but by the grace of God, their town and family had not yet been affected. It was a fact that the pogroms would be coming closer and the attacks more violent. In every town the Cossacks emtered they destroyed everything in their path. The inhabitants quickly got off the streets, because they did want not be trampled by horses, killed by swinging swords, or hit by flying bullets. When the Cossacks camped nearby, they often got drunk and would look for young girls to rape, young men to push around, and homes to pillage. When this occurred, Leib and his family would often hide in the crawl space under the floorboards of their house until the threat was over. If the house were to be set on fire, like so many others, they would likely unable to escape and all burn to death. The whole family knew if they were able survive today's threat, there was always the threat of tomorrow. It had become more and more difficult for the family to find safe hiding places. Very often they were forced to spend many days hiding in the forest without food or water. The family began to keep a small amount of supplies hidden in a hollowed out tree trunk for such an emergency. Often it was not enough to take them through the cold nights and long days.

It had gotten so dangerous it was no longer safe to conduct any organized services in the Temple. The study of Torah and prayers had to be said in secret, and in small gatherings. Often the small groups would meet in closed businesses after hours and in people homes. There was no doubt in Heshel's mind that the time had come for him to leave Russia for America. When he told his parents, they did not like the idea, and disagreed with his decision. He explained that he was young and healthy enough for the journey, and it would give them one less person to feed. Leib and Fanny kept thinking about him leaving, and knew for him to leave was the only way they could protect him, so they agreed to let him go. Heshel was not yet sixteen. With a heavy heart and the fear of never seeing her first born child again, Fanny helped Heshel get ready to leave. She gave him a warm sweater she had just finished knitting, some black bread, a few onions, and some small fresh baked cookies.

Heshel's trip out of Zhitomir took him through St. Petersburg, then over the Baltic Sea down through to Germany and finally to Antwerp, Belgium. It took Heshel more than three monthss to travel from Russia to Belgium, a distance of nearly twelve hundred miles. Heshel covered usually ten to twelve miles a day, most of the time not knowing where he was. The lessons that Heshel had learned as a young child helped keep him hidden and safe on his journey. It was a hard and difficult trip walking day and night. Now and then though Heshel would come across a group of travelers and be allowed to ride for a while in the back of a wagon pulled by an Ox.

Heshel followed the stars by night and road signs by day. The time Heshel had spent out in the fields as a young boy learning about the land instead of learning Torah was paying off. He had learned which berries and plants could be eaten and which would kill him. The only food he had was what grew in the forests, the fields and the shoulders of the road. He also knew how to treat a wound and stop a fever, because for years his father had harped on about things that could save one's life on a long journey. One day, while trying to sleep between some fallen trees and under a blanket of leaves, three soldiers on patrol found him. They pulled him from his hiding place and started to push him around. But Heshel was young, strong, and very fast, so when one of the soldiers stumbled, Heshel made a break and ran deeper into the woods. He took them all by surprise and he was gone before they even knew what had happened. Heshel then climbed up a tree and as the soldiers approached he held his breath. Because the soldiers were so stupid they never bothered to look up. After this incident Heshel knew playtime was over, and he knew if they found him, he would be shot on the spot. While in the tree, it had started to rain and there was no moon or stars to help him navigate. He decided to rest until the rain stopped. After about two hours, the storm subsided, and there was no sight or sound of any more patrols. Heshel then came down out of the tree and ran until he could run no more.

It took a little over three months for Heshel to reach the seaport in Antwerp, Belgium. This same trip today would take only about four days by car. Heshel was excited over reaching Belgium. But he now faced another problem: he needed to find boat transportation to get to America. Heshel had no money for passage, so he decided he would try to get a job onboard one of the vessels sailing to America. Heshel asked around the Antwerp docks trying to find a job on a ship bound for America. At first he had no luck securing work on any ship sailing where he needed to go. After many rejections, he finally found a ship heading for the east coast of the United States, and it was due to sail later that same day. When he found the captain, Heshel begged for a job. "I won't be any trouble, and I will eat very little." The captain liked the spunk of this young man standing before him. After a short deliberation, he told young Heshel, "You can work off your passage. I can't afford to pay you; but we'll feed you and if you survive the voyage you will get to America." After thanking the captain, Heshel grabbed his things and started up the gang plank. As he got halfway up he said a short prayer. "Dear God, please take care of my family, and I hope I see them again." After the ship cast off and put out to sea, for the first time Heshel started to believe that he might yet make it to freedom, but he also knew he would never see the land of his birth again. Although it had only been about three months, he already missed his family especially his baby sister Ida who was almost twelve.

Life on a ship in July of 1911 was not a pleasant joyride and was filled with danger. Many of the passengers were without the money to pay for a place on deck let alone the luxury of a stateroom. All their worldly belongings were either carried with them or for the lucky few in a steamer trunk. Heshel did what was asked of him aboard ship and never once complained. This included disposing the dead bodies of passengers that died during the voyage. Each night Heshel fell into his bunk with every bone and muscle in his body hurting. With all the heavy work, sickness, and small amount of food, on board he endured a difficult journey. Heshel did not believe he would ever live to see his new home in America. It was sweltering hot during the day and very cold at night, but unlike many of the poor passengers Heshel was fortunate he had a place to sleep out of the weather and a blanket to put over him at night. As the ship steamed into New York harbor, the captain pointed out the Statue of Liberty to Heshel who was so happy he immediately thanked God for his safe arrival and then broke down into tears. It was August 1910 and all the work, pain, and agony his fifteen-year-old body had endured was almost at an end, as he had finally arrived in America, the place he dreamed of as a young boy.

Every immigrant's new beginning started on a three acre island in New York Harbor. Like so many that arrived before and after him, Heshel's processing started at a counter in the island's main hall. From 1892 to 1954, twelve million immigrants were processed on Ellis Island. The numbers would have been higher, but if you were found to be ill, you were detained; if you had no place to go you were detained; if you were too old or too young, you were detained, and some were sent back to the country from where they started. Many children were held because their parents had died on the way over and they needed to find a relative or orphanage before they could be released from the island. Just because you made it to Ellis Island did not mean you would make it to shore.

Another problem for most of the people arriving was they did not speak English. This slowed down the processing of paperwork. In Heshel's case he only spoke Russian and Yiddish and would have had a difficult time communicating with the staff at Ellis Island. But Heshel was one of the lucky ones, because the Immigration Officer (a woman) that processed him also spoke Yiddish. Heshel explained that he had a sister named Leah, living in Brooklyn and then showed her a piece of paper that he brought with him all the way from Russia. Written in Yiddish was the name and address of his sister. After all the paperwork was done, somehow Heshel Rabinowitz became "Harry Rubin." Young Heshel was not at first aware of the name-change. Many families lost their true names while entering this strange new land; and were not aware of it until it was done and they had left the island.

After arriving in America in 1905, Leah and her husband Isaac Modell settled in Williamsburg, Brooklyn. With the help of strangers, Harry finally found his way to the apartment where they lived. He knocked on the door and prayed his sister and her family still lived there. When Leah answered the knock and opened the door she just stared at the young man in front of her. The last time she had seen Heshel, he had been a young boy of nine, and now she was looking at a man of fifteen. When Harry smiled and said, "Shalom, Leah." Leah saw the smile of the little brother, who she never dreamed of seeing again. She screamed, cried, and hugged her little brother, right in the middle of the hallway. For the first time in his life, Heshel finally felt safe. Before doing anything, Leah decided the first thing she should do was to introduce her brother to his nephew Harry born in December 1906 and his niece Frieda born in May 1909. She then fixed something for Heshel to eat. While he ate, Leah continued to ask him question after question about his trip. She could not get enough of listening to him talk about how the family was, how he managed to get on a ship, and how he made it out of Russia.

Heshel told Leah about the latest news of the family, which by this time was more than three months old. They both knew that there was no way of knowing how they were currently doing. Leah's husband Isaac came home to find quite a pleasant surprise. His young brother-in-law had arrived, and the story of his escape was told yet again. It was then Leah and Isaac looked at his paperwork from Ellis Island. Leah and Isaac then told him that his name had been changed from Heshel Rabinowitz to Harry Rubin. He was not sure what to make of it, but he thought it seemed to feel right. He had a new name for a new life in a new country. Leah fixed Harry a hot bath. It was the first one he could remember in a long time. Meanwhile she set-up the couch for him to sleep on. Within minutes he was fast asleep without having to listen for the Cossacks or the screams and crying of sick or dying people on the ship. This was the first peaceful night's sleep he had in a very long time.

The first job Harry had in his new home was working for a mattress company and earning just two dollars a week. He kept one dollar for himself and gave one to Leah for room and board. It was the least he could do while he was living with her and Isaac in their apartment. Harry worked from sun-up until dark. It was a very hot fall this particular year. The temperatures in New York were over one hundred degrees. Harry had to schlep a wagon full of mattresses all over Brooklyn. It was difficult for him to maneuver around the pushcart vendors and the local residents milling around the streets and sidewalks. Harry thought, "Why do all these people have to be in my way?"

The new hardship was to endure the crowds and ill tempered customers. It made the work on the ship seem like a piece of cake. The difference was that in New York he got to eat every day and sleep on a soft couch, and he felt safe. After a few months of doing this Harry knew one thing: he needed a new job, and he needed it sooner rather than later. While he worked like a dog during the day, Leah worked with him late into the night. To succeed in this new land he needed to be able to read, write and speak the English language. Harry was always very smart and was a quick learner. He was happy to be with Leah and Isaac but he was lonely and missed the rest of his family. He knew that at the rate he was able to save money now he would never see them again.

Harry was always thinking, "I need to get a better paying job, I need to get a better paying job, and I need to get a better paying job!" It was the mantra that played in his mind day in and day out. One day when he was making one of his mattress deliveries he passed a store, and in the front window, there was a sign with the picture of a man in a white and blue top hat and a red white and blue suit. The man was pointing a finger directly at Harry and underneath the picture were printed in large bold letters the words I WANT YOU FOR U.S. ARMY.

Another sign said, "Help protect your country and join the Army now!" Harry kept on walking but now he was thinking, *"Maybe this is what I need to do."* He kept making his mattress deliveries and kept on thinking it's got to be better than this. One day after his last delivery Harry made his way back to the Army recruiting office and walked in and asked what he had to do to sign up. He never even asked what he would be paid. He just knew it had to be more than he was making now. When he left the office fifteen minutes later, he felt wonderful. In spite of the heat he ran all the way home to tell Leah about what he had done. This was going to be an easy way out and Harry was on top of the world. He had still not yet turned sixteen.

Harry burst into the apartment and in one long breath he shouted, "I just joined up and I'm in the Army now. I report to camp in three days. Isn't that great?" His sister was not happy to hear that Harry had joined the army. She finally had him safe and now he was going to put himself in danger again. All Harry kept telling her was about the places he would get to see, the adventures he would go on, and the money he would make. The United States had not yet joined the war. He really thought this opportunity would be wonderful. Harry told Leah, "Look, if I could live through pogroms and a sea voyage under the worst conditions, then how bad could it be in the army?" As he continued he said, "I will be able to see the world, make money, and send for the rest of the family." Harry went on to tell his sister he would no longer be a burden to her and Isaac. All Harry had on his mind was that he would be able to send for the family faster. They had gotten a letter just about a month earlier that said they were all still alive which seemed to be a miracle. But things could have gotten even worse in Russia in the interim.

War was brewing in Europe and it was all everyone spoke about. In the U.S.A. you had to be eighteen to sign up for the armed services. It had been easy for Harry to convince the recruiter that he was eighteen because he had been through so much in his short life and he looked much older than he really was. The journey across Russia, the work on the ship and the mattress job had aged him.

After signing up, Harry felt a weight had been lifted from his shoulders. He now had a purpose, was a certified soldier and had a way to earn money for his family. When he left three days later, he was just like a little boy going out to play in the sunshine. He was all excited and ready for a new adventure.

Harry spent his first year and sixteenth birthday in Army Basic Training in Louisiana. He was not sure how much he liked the South, because it was like no place he had ever been before. He was not used to the southern drawl people spoke. All the English he knew had a Brooklyn/Yiddish lilt to it. Harry was a hard worker and did very well in basic training. He wanted to be the very best soldier he could be. He knew one day it might save his life. He wanted to learn all there was to know about fighting and surviving. He had all the instincts. He just needed the training to bring them out.

When he had left Russia, he was a young boy without very much knowledge on how to protect himself or his family. Now he was learning. He was learning the Army way. At night he would fall onto his bed exhausted. When reveille sounded at five a.m. every morning, most soldiers did not have a good night's rest. It was a annoying for everyone to have to wake -up to the sound of a bugle blasting and the Drill Instructor singing "YOU GOTTA GET UP, YOU GOTTA GET UP, YOU GOTTA GET UP IN THE MORNING." It really rubbed Harry the wrong way getting up so early because it was always so dark out when reveille played. The darkness always made him feel that he should still be sleeping.

It was not long before most of the members of his platoon found out that Harry was Jewish. But other members of the platoon found out the hard way that he was no one to trifle with. It was very rare in those days to find Jews in the armed forces. First, the army could not meet their Jewish Kosher dietary needs. The cooks in the Army were mostly gentile, and they had no clue how to fix a kosher meal. There was another reason Jews had a difficult time being in the military. It was the same reason most gentiles in main street America did not much care for them. It was always believed that Jews were not fighters. Harry and other Jewish soldiers in the U.S. Army were exceptions who surprised everyone and fought to win for America.

Harry had lived through the pogroms in Russia. Stepping off that boat to America, he did not expect the same treatment of the Jewish population in the US. Harry found the same anti-Semitism and remarks like "Jews, where are your horns? I thought all Jews had horns." He even heard the derogatory comments of the servicemen calling Jews "kikes" or "dirty Jews." He expected that in Russia but not in the United States. So Harry made a decision. He would not put up with name-calling or any other disrespect by anti-Semites.

Harry decided to take action which often meant he got into a fist fight, which in turn ended him in military stockade or solitary confinement. He was placed there more than once for his fighting. Harry soon learned to hold his temper at least until he was off base. If a fight took place off base, there was less of a chance of ending up in the stockade.

Harry had a bunkmate named Tom. Tom was a foot taller than Harry and at least fifty pounds heavier. Tom came from a small town in the deep South where there were no Jews. Because of this, he knew nothing about Harry and his beliefs. Most of what he learned was from his bigoted family. Tom had been brought up to believe that Jews killed Jesus Christ and that all Jews were sneaky and not to be trusted.

Tom made the mistake of picking on Harry one too many times. Harry got so angry one day he could no longer take the name-calling and wise-cracks and he and Tom ended up in a fight. After that fight, they became the best of friends. Tom thought, "Hell, if he can beat me up, he can't be all that bad, and I want him fighting with me, not against me."

After a few more fights with other platoon members all the men learned to respect Harry for who he was. In fact, the guys in his platoon really liked his spunk. They decided that they would rather be his friend than his enemy. Soon they all found out that he could drink with the best of them and whenever there was a bar-brawl Harry's side always won.

After a year of basic training, Harry was ready to see the world. The assignment his platoon received was security duty in the Panama Canal Zone. Before he left for Panama, he made sure his sister Leah had the money she needed to send for the rest of the family. He did not know what would happen once you entered the assignment area. Harry was determined that even if he never made it back to American soil, he would keep his promise to get all of his family out of harm's way. Harry was shipped out to Panama before he knew if his family ever received the money he had saved for them. He did not even know if they would be able to leave Russia.

The Panama Canal Project was begun by the French in 1881. Under French control the work was compromised by widespread government corruption, red tape, crooked vendors, antiquated equipment, unsanitary conditions, numerous diseases native to the area and a high accident mortality rate. French canal excavation operations were abandoned in 1888.

In 1904, the United States bought the construction rights. The U.S. believed that discoveries in the first few years of the 20th century could provide better control over all aspects of the project, allowing workers to move more soil and to build the canal at a substantially faster rate. In 1914 when Harry was deployed to Panama it was his job to try to help keep the peace there. The purpose of the canal was to make it possible for cargo ships to cross between the Atlantic and Pacific Oceans in a matter of twenty to thirty hours. Without the canal the trip down around Cape Horn and back up along either coast is about eight thousand miles longer.

The U.S. Government thought it very important for naval vessels to be able to cross from one ocean to the other as quickly and safely as possible in the event of a war in Europe.

The biggest problem slowing progress on the canal project for both France and the U.S. was the lack of sanitary living and working conditions in the encampments. Yellow fever and malaria were both spread by the large numbers of the ever present mosquito. The poor sanitary conditions would have to be solved immediately to stop soldiers from getting infected. The lack of an adequate infection control allowed disease to kill many soldiers, native workers, and civilian contractors. So not only was the Army responsible to keep the peace; they had to find a method to eradicate the medical problems that put the project in jeopardy. Another problem was the lack of anything for the men to do during their time off. Usually they spent most non-working hours in saloons which led to brawls and physical injuries of all sorts. As time passed, Harry had made many friends in his platoon. But it was very hard for him to watch those friends suffering and dying from malaria and yellow fever or drinking themselves sick.

As time passed for Harry in Panama he rose up the ranks fast. He was a natural born leader, set a good example, and was quickly promoted to Sergeant. Meanwhile the Rabinowitz family was in Zhitomir preparing for their trip to America. They would be allowed only one trunk for the five of them, so it was with a heavy heart they picked and chose what would stay and what would go. Some clothing for the long journey, dried food, a few pictures to remember loved ones left behind. They had to take Leib's Tallit (prayer shawl) and Fanny's brass candlesticks. They dressed in as many layers of clothing as they could to make room for other things in the trunk. But the family had to leave Morris, his wife Shandel (Jennie), and Dora and her husband behind.

The family traveled to Antwerp, Belgium, which is the embarkation point for the ships to America. Heshel made the same trip five years earlier. But he did not have the financial resources that Leib and Fanny and the children now had. They were able to book passage where Heshel had to work on a ship in exchange for passage.

In early September 1914, the family boarded the S.S. Kroonland. The Kroonland was bound for Ellis Island in New York Harbor, in a place called the United States of America. The Kroonland was built in 1902 by the Red Star Line. Once the ship left Belgium, Leib and his family never looked back. They were full of hope that they would soon see Leah and the rest of the family again. They had no idea what life would be like in this country they were heading for.

By now Fanny and Leib had been married nineteen years. The hard life they lived had taken its toll on both of them. They were hopeful the new beginning would make them feel young again. In their heart of hearts, they prayed that the life in America would bring a new sense of safety and freedom for their family.

After enduring twenty days of bad weather, rough seas, and a brief boarding by the British Navy, the family finally sailed past the statue of liberty into New York harbor, were disembarked from the Kroonland to Ellis Island on October 14, 1914, and went through the same processing that Heshel went through years earlier. There was a great deal of paperwork amd also a few name changes. Albert Rabinowitz became Al Rubin and Yankel Rabinowitz became Jack Rubin. For unknown reasons Leib, Fanny, and Ida were the only family members to keep the last name Rabinowitz.

Once everyone was cleared by immigration they were met at the exit gate by Leah and Isaac. After a brief and joyous reunion they were taken straight to the apartment that Leah had been able to get for them. The apartment was on Siegel Street in Williamsburg, Brooklyn. It was a four room railroad flat. The rooms were all off a long hallway just like in a railroad sleeper car. It was more than they could have ever wished for. There was one window in the back of the apartment, which overlooked a cement courtyard with garbage cans over-flowing with rotting food and swarms of flies all around -- a stench they had never encountered before. The front of the apartment more than made up for the back. The two front windows faced a lovely street with trees and a little patch of grass. There was very little space between big buildings, and many families living in them. There were more people living in a two block area than had lived in their whole town in Russia. All this would take some getting used to. There were no forests, streams, or people that they knew walking around. They traded space and fresh air for a life without pogroms and fear.

In America, they had no fear of gun shots or bombs. All they heard were the quiet sounds of a new homeland. The boys were most taken with the iron fire escape. It was something they had never seen before and were climbing out the window to play on it before anyone could stop them. They begged their parents to be allowed to sleep on it at night. Their parents finally gave in; so the boys took the blankets Leah had given them and slept under the stars. The next day on the street outside the apartment there were people milling around and speaking Russian, Yiddish, Polish, and English. The family was amazed that the people all seemed to be getting along with one another. Leib and Fanny had lived most of their lives in terrible poverty. For the first time they were beginning to relax and feel that maybe they would be able to live out the rest of their lives in peace. Also they began to believe that the dreams they had in Russia would maybe come true. Two hours after they arrived at the apartment the boys were out on the streets making new friends. They were learning some new English words. As boys will be boys, the first words they learned were not words they could repeat in front of their parents. The whole family went to sleep that first evening with joy in their hearts and expectations for the next day.

Leib left early to see what kind of work would be available in a Synagogue within walking distance. While walking the streets Leib met some people in the neighborhood who were from Zhitomir and other neighboring towns in Russia. They helped him find his way around just as he would later help others. Leib figured it would take him only a few days to become familiar with his surroundings. One night he returned home with a light in his eyes that no one had seen for a very long time. He walked over to Fanny picked her up and gave her a big kiss, which shocked her as well as the kids. Fanny said, "Leib, what has gotten into you." Leib just smiled and said, "I have been in this wonderful new country only a few days and I have already found a job." "Tell us all about it," everyone yelled at one time. "Well I was walking around the neighborhood looking for a Synagogue we could pray in, and I found one right here in Williamsburg. I met the Rabbi and we got to talking, and I told him we just arrived in America and I was a Cantor and a teacher and I needed a job. He thought for a moment and hired me on the spot." "How wonderful!" Fanny shouted and there was more hugging and kissing going around. Leib said "The best part is it pays $9 a week, and soon we will be rich! The boys will go to school in the morning to learn to read and write English. Then they could work in the afternoons and in the evening, I will teach them and the other boys Torah. What more could a man ask for?"

Soon after arriving in New York, Jack was able to get an afternoon job. He worked as a delivery boy for a bakery and earned two dollars a week. Al also found a job earning a dollar and a half delivering the *Jewish Daily Forward*, a newspaper which is still in print today. With Al, Jack and Lieb working, the family was making $12.50 a week, a small fortune in those days. Harry had been able to get only a few letters from home, but he knew that his parents and some of his family had arrived safely in America. Little by little the family was able to buy some furniture. The first items they bought were three beds. The boys shared one bed; one was for Ida, and the third was for Leib and Fanny. They also bought a dining table with six chairs, an icebox, curtains, linoleum, and some mirrors. This took them only a few months to accomplish and they felt like they were living like royalty. They all loved their new life in America, and the best part was that there were no pogroms. Fanny was now able to visit with Leah and Isaac and the grandchildren and most important they were able to share Shabbat together, something Fanny never dreamed would happen during those bad years in Zhitomir.

As time passed from late 1914 to mid 1915, unknown to everyone, it was going to be a great year. Many wonderful things were going to happen for the Rubin family. In less than one year's time there was finally enough money saved between Harry's Army pay and the earnings of Leib, Jack, and Al to send for the rest of the family that remained in Russia. Left behind were Harry's older brother Morris, his wife Shandel (Jennie), and Harry's older sister Dora and her family. In the end they too were brought to America and all were happy and finally together in Brooklyn. The only person missing was Harry, who was in Panama serving in the Army.

In late 1915 while his whole family was settling into their new home, Harry was enduring more and more danger and hardship in Panama. The army was charged with the protection of the construction workers and civilians. The tragic aspect of being in the Canal Zone was watching more and more of his friends get sick and die. Somehow, Harry managed to keep fit and out of harm's way. It had been three years since he joined the army and he was able finally to get a two-week furlough to go home to Brooklyn. This would be the first time in almost five years he would see his parents and siblings in one place.

Fanny and Leib were in Williamsburg and that's the first place Harry went when he got off the boat from Panama in New York Harbor. He walked up the steps to their first floor apartment and knocked on the door. His heart was beating so fast that he thought he would pass out before the knock was answered. Fanny was just finishing up cleaning the apartment for the start of the Sabbath, and did not hear the first knock. She was busy putting newspapers on the clean kitchen floor. The windows sparkled, the table was set, and the Sabbath candles were in the brass candle sticks all shiny and ready to be lit. Harry was anxious with anticipation as he knocked again and again getting a little impatient, trying not to break down the door. As he tried to stand still he took a deep breath, and he caught the smell of his mother's homemade chicken soup and fresh baked challis in the air, which had an instant powerful effect on him, and suddenly he banged on the door with all his might "Who is it?" yelled Fanny. "Don't you know it's almost Shabbat?" As she opened the door, a dish towel in one hand, Harry's baby-sister Ida walked in from the back bedroom to see what all the fuss was about. As soon as she saw it was her big brother; she ran across the room and jumped right into his arms.

Fanny stood looking at this grown man and all she could see was her baby boy. She screamed and cried, held her hand to her heart. Then she stepped across the door threshold and fell into Harry's waiting arms. Fanny had always had the fear that she would never see her beloved son Heshel again. She had known he had made it to America and that he was now deployed to Panama. She never thought she would once again hold him in her arms. Tears streamed down her cheeks, and he kissed them all away. "Heshel, you're home!" she cried as she buried her face and wet tears into his shoulder. "Heshel Heshel Oh my God, how wonderful. Wait until Papa and the boys see you!"

Harry held onto his mother and baby sister and walked them back over the threshold into the apartment and closed the door. He was having a hard a time believing that he was actually in his mother's house and that everyone was safe. Because he had gotten to see his family again whatever happened to him when he returned to Panama would be easier to live with. He was also thinking about how much older his mother looked since he had seen her four years earlier. But she looked healthier than he ever remembered seeing her before. Just then he heard the front door open and shut. It was Leib, Al, and Jack returning from Synagogue. After the door closed they heard Fanny crying in the kitchen. They hurried to find out the reason. To their surprise they found Heshel trying to comfort his mother and sister and trying to drink the glass of hot tea Fanny was forcing on him. Heshel jumped up to embrace his father and brothers.

Meanwhile Leib offered up a prayer, "Dear God, you have answered my prayers and sent back my son, I will forever be in your debt."

Leib asked "Can it really be over four years since I have seen you my son?"

The last time he had seen his son he was a frightened skinny fifteen year old boy. Now he was a twenty year old man who stood in front of him looking handsome and strong in his army uniform. The pride Leib felt for his son just beamed from his face and lit up the room.

Leib wished Harry would serve his time in the Army and get out before the United States got into the war raging in Europe. Leib felt his son had served in enough personal wars for a lifetime and had earned the right to some rest. Leib knew Harry was different from the rest of his children. Torah and being a devout Jew was not his calling in life. The year on the run and the three years he had been in the service had not allowed him to keep kosher and it made no difference to him. Leib just hoped that being back among his own kind again Heshel might find a nice Jewish girl from a good religious home, and settle down with the right woman and have a family who would bring him back to his Jewish roots.

On Saturday night when Shabbat was over Fanny and Ida still had to clean the table and wash the dishes. Leib suggested that he and the boys take Heshel and go to the Turkish baths. Heshel thought this sounded very relaxing. Besides he was not used to being idle for such a long time and was more than ready to stretch his legs. As they walked down the block towards the Turkish baths, the locals noticed that Cantor Rabinowitz was walking with a soldier. They knew right away that he was Leib's son Heshel. Leib had told all of the local residents at Temple that Heshel was coming home on leave. The Cantor and his sons were stopped many times along the way by members of Leib's congregation and the local neighbors that were out walking around and visiting with one another. The locals also heard how brave Heshel was and everyone that saw them wanted to stop and shake his hand and welcome him home.

Much the same thing happened inside the Turkish baths. Everyone Heshel met told him that they would pray for his safe return. After they had left the apartment for the Turkish baths the rest of the family slowly arrived. First Morris with his wife Shandel, then Dora and her husband, then Leah and Isaac with their two kids. About an hour later, Lieb, Al, Jack and Heshel returned from the Turkish bath very refreshed. As they walked into the apartment Fanny and Ida were telling everyone how handsome and grown-up Heshel was.

That night the whole family sat around in the living room talking late. They asked Heshel about his adventures in the Army. He told them where he had traveled – Canada, France, England and finally Panama -- but he skimmed over the troubles he had seen. He left out not having much to eat, watching men die all around him, and living in filthy toxic conditions. The less the family knew; he decided, the better off they would be.

In response the family told Heshel about developments in their lives. Al and Jack were still living at home. Although they were no longer in school, they were working full time to help the family. Jack now looked at his older brother with awe. He had been only thirteen when Heshel left Russia. Jack had wanted to travel with him, but Heshel knew it would be safer to travel alone, and Jack had to be left behind.

Jack remembered a time when he and Heshel were children in Russia. Jack had fallen into a fast moving river swollen from heavy rains and Heshel jumped in and used all his strength to save his younger brother. Jack would never forget what his older brother did for him.

Soon after Heshel left home in Russia, his older brother, Morris met a wonderful girl by the name of Shandel (Jennie). A few months after meeting, they married and were very happy together. In America Morris went into the mattress business.

Heshel took a long look at his baby sister Ida. Now she was a beautiful young girl of fifteen.

He thought of all the troubles his family had to endure after he left. It upset him that he was not there to help. He decided that when he was out of the military, he would do everything he could to make it up to them.

After everyone had left, Heshel got ready for bed. Fanny set up a feather-bed in the back room for her boy. He slept without fear in the safety of his parent's home. The last time he had seen them he had been a skinny, scared boy running for his life. Three years later, he was a grown man protecting America, his new homeland. The next morning the smell of his favorite cookies baking woke Harry up at nine a.m. It was a much more pleasant way to wake up than hearing an obnoxious bugle at five a.m.

Fanny fed Heshel breakfast. While he ate, she set up the tub in the kitchen. She also left the stove on so it would stay warm in the apartment. Then Fanny and Ida left to go shopping so Heshel could have his bath in privacy.

The next two weeks flew by quickly. Harry spent his time with family and friends and did as much as he could to enjoy himself. World War I was raging all over Europe and he was still stationed in Panama. Heshel knew the chances of his seeing his family again were slim. So he decided to make the most of the time he had left. The whole family was there at the pier when Heshel boarded the ship to return to Panama. As the ship started pulling away from the dock, Heshel was very sad. It was really hard leaving his family again, but at least this time, he knew they were safe at last.

With his furlough behind him, it was back to the Army for Harry. He spent the next six years trying to keep out trouble. Harry was very good at what he did. He was a born leader, and everyone respected him. During his years in the service, Harry rose from Private First Class through the ranks to Sergeant. In 1917 while the war in Europe raged on, Harry was still in the Panama Canal Zone and the living conditions were still extremely bad. There was no decent sanitation available, and it was no surprise that there was always some disease outbreak of one kind or another. For several years Harry was able stay healthy by keeping himself and his possessions as clean as possible, but in the long run even this could not keep him safe. One day while he was in the field on maneuvers he was struck with a high fever and a terrible case of malaria. Somehow he managed to get back to the base.

He crawled through many miles of jungle before passing out just outside the front gate of the base almost dead. An MP who was walking the perimeter found Harry lying on the ground unconscious. The MP called the medics and just may have saved Harry's life. A week later Harry woke up in a hospital. All around him were the coffins of fellow soldiers who were not as lucky as he. It looked like God was still watching out for him.

While he was recuperating, he received a letter from home. It was bad news. His beloved baby sister Ida had died from pneumonia. This was almost more than he could bear. Ida was only nineteen when she died. She left behind a husband, Benjamin, and a three year old son, Heshel, who was called Heshy. Since Benjamin suffered from polio and was confined to a wheel-chair, the care of Heshy was left to Fanny and Leib. This was hard on them, as they were getting older, but they managed as best as they could.

Leib and the family were looking for a piece of the American dream. The dream was finally realized when Al and Jack entered into a partnership and bought a chicken market on Staten Island.

In November 18, 1918, the war in Europe ended and Sergeant Harry Rubin returned to the United States. He was assigned as an Army Recruiter in Georgia. By this time he had spent four years in the Army, had served with distinction and he might have applied for a discharge, but he decided to stay in a little longer. And this he did until 1922 when he decided that since the whole family had now been brought over from the old country, it was time at last to do something for himself.

Things were changing in America. Women were becoming more independent. It was now acceptable to marry for love and not because someone arranged a blending of two families. Harry wondered what life would be like without the discipline of being in the Army.

All sorts of things ran through his mind. Would he ever meet a woman who would understand him and his wild ways? He knew that he could not become a devout Jew and live under his parent's roof. Since he had lived his life protecting his family, now he wanted to live a little for himself. He wondered what kind of job he would find. One thing he did know: a job in his brother's chicken market was not an option. So far things had gone his way and he hoped they would continue to do so. He needed something that would challenge him. In the end he decided he would just have to see what fate had in store.

ROSE'S FAMILY

After arriving in America, Rebecca and Nathan decided to start a family. In January of 1906 Nathan and Rebecca welcomed into the world their first child, a boy they named Frank. He was a beautiful baby and big for his age. Eleven months later on December 19, 1906, Rebecca delivered her second child. The labor was difficult. When contractions started, the pain was so great that Rebecca screamed and yelled and thought she would die. Between contractions the midwife tried to be reassuring, saying the pain would soon be over and soon Rebecca would be able to hold a new life in her hands. As the contractions came harder and harder she asked herself, "Wasn't this supposed to get easier with the second child?"

In the end she gave birth to a daughter named Annie. This was a blessing, for a daughter was just what Nathan and Rebecca had wanted.

The midwife cleaned up Rebecca and the baby and then allowed Nathan and baby Frank to enter. They were thrilled beyond words and could not believe how beautiful the baby was. Soon the midwife shooed Nathan and little Frank out of the room as Rebecca needed to rest. Even the midwife, who had helped bring hundreds of babies into the world, was taken with the beauty of this baby girl. The midwife cooed to the baby as she worked on cleaning her up. "What a beautiful little girl you are and how lucky you are to have a big brother to look after you." Meanwhile Rebecca rested and Nathan went to the Synagogue to thank God for this miracle of new life.

A few years later, in 1910, Rebecca gave birth to a second son, Simon, and then two years later a third son, Jack. Rebecca thought Jack would be her last but eight years later she was to give birth to one more child, Emil, also known as Jerry.

Nathan and Rebecca had been very lucky. They were able to escape from Poland soon after they had been married. It was a blessing that all their children would be born in America. Rebecca and Nathan were so proud when they came through Ellis Island. Upon release from immigration custody they headed straight for Brooklyn, where many friends from their hometown had settled. First and foremost in their minds was that they were now able to practice their religion without fear of persecution. Also there were no pogroms and there was an equal chance for everyone to make a living. In Poland Nathan had been a poor farmer and was just barely able to feed his parents and young wife but in America life was good and eventually he was able to rear four healthy sons and a beautiful daughter.

Nathan and Rebecca were overjoyed with Annie. She brought light into their lives. She had porcelain white skin, dark eyes, and jet black hair. Whenever her mother took her out for a stroll, people would stop and comment on the beauty of the child. Life was good for the Cohen family. Rebecca cooked and cleaned the apartment, and Nathan went to the Synagogue to pray and study, as Jewish law commanded. At Nathan's insistence, the boys received a good education and learned Hebrew. Nathan also expected his sons to be part of the Jewish community. This was very important to him. Nathan always told the children: "You must never forget who you are and where you come from." He felt that being devout and doing what was commanded by Jewish law was the least a man could do to prove to God that he was truly grateful for all he had been given in life.

Nathan was very strict. In his opinion, a woman's duty was to bear children and take care of the home and the needs of the men in the family. For Orthodox women, life was harsh. Young girls were taught at an early age to sew, cook and clean. Few young women received an education since being educated was not a necessity for a wife and mother. Even today, although they have more say about their lives, not much has changed for women in Orthodox homes. Today a woman is permitted to have a job but only because this allows the men to study the Torah on a daily basis. After work the women are still responsible for taking care of the husband, children, and home.

In most Jewish homes, family was the center of everyone's life. Families sat down to a home cooked meal together every night, and talked about the events of the day. On Sundays, family members often traveled to the homes of their relatives. Everyone looked forward to these outings. It was the time you got to see grandparents, parents, brothers, sisters, aunts and uncles. For the children, it was a time to play with cousins. Families would take turns hosting the Sunday get- together, so the burden of entertaining would not fall on one family. Family members rarely moved very far away from one another and, if you started early, in one day you could visit relatives in the Bronx, Queens and Brooklyn. The younger generation was expected to visit the older members of the family and although those were hard times, a grandfather or uncle might slip you a piece of fruit, some nuts, a piece of candy, or even a few pennies.

The apartment Annie grew up in was rather dreary. Rebecca did not have the knack for making it look homey and cheerful. To see the sunshine Annie had to go to the kitchen window and look over the top of the building next door. Sometimes Annie would go up to the roof and pretend she lived in the country surrounded by flowers. Other times she would imagine that she was a princess in a tower, waiting for her prince.

Annie was usually nicely dressed and her hair beautifully combed. She had two loving parents and four over-protective brothers watching out for her. She grew up loving everything around her -- the sun, the sky and school. Most of all she loved her parents and her brothers. Even though they did tease her unmercifully, still she loved them.

Annie felt very lucky to have such a perfect life, especially when her father Nathan came home every night. Annie always ran to greet him at the door. Nathan's big blue eyes twinkled with joy every time he looked at his daughter. He always had something to give her such as a penny or piece of candy hidden in his pocket. Sometimes it was just a funny joke. Whatever it was Annie always looked forward to her father coming home. He would often take the time to hold her on his lap and tell stories or sing silly songs.

Annie just adored her father and in his eyes she could do no wrong. It was Nathan who started her calling her brother Frank "frankfurter." When she called him that, she would always burst out laughing. He would take the time to hold Annie on his lap and just to tell her stories or sing her silly songs he had learned as a child.

It wasn't until she was about eight years old that she realized that everything in her perfect world was really not so perfect. She now had a wider circle of friends and places she was allowed to go and visit. She realized that her home was really shabby compared to the homes of her friends. Then she realized that Rebecca was really not a good housekeeper and that it had nothing to do with the lack of money.

Annie and her brothers did not often mind one little bit or did not seem to be bothered by the constant bickering that had started between their parents. The darkness of the apartment and the fighting and constant bickering between Nathan and Rebecca made it a place of despair. All this bothered Annie and her brothers a great deal. Rebecca always seemed to be nagging Nathan about everything and anything. The reason she nagged was Nathan spent so much time engrossed with playing cards with his sons, reading or praying, and paid little attention to the day to day happenings of his wife or Annie. Rebecca was always exhausted all the time from her boring daily routine of cooking, shopping, and caring for a large family. She never had the time to just sit and read or relax and do nothing or visit with friends.

During Shabbat dinner Nathan would sit at the head of the table during Shabbat dinner because he was head of the family. The family would follow him in prayer. Emil (Jerry), the youngest son of Nathan's four sons was the one most interested in prayer and learning the Torah and Talmud. Nathan was most proud of Emil (Jerry). Nathan was always showing Emil's religious talents off at the Synagogue every week.

To escape the troubles at home Annie occupied her time just sitting outside on the front stoop and watching people walk by. Annie loved going to school and would just love when the weekend ended. She walked about seven blocks to grammar school every day. As she walked, she engaged in her favorite pastime, people-watching. She watched them rushing to their various morning jobs and chores. She watched the mailman on his route and wondered how he got all the mail in that big bag every day. She watched the men on their way to Shul and the women going to the pushcarts to start bargaining for the day's produce. Annie's favorite thing to watch was the fire trucks and the men on them. Often Annie would try to chase a speeding fire truck just to see where it was going. With her little heart beating and her little legs pumping, she ran as fast as she could in order to keep up. She just loved the thrill of it all. Anything was better than her humdrum life. The excitement of the fire, the firemen with their hoses spurting out water, the people screaming for help, all held a hidden thrill for her.

One day after school, Annie saw a fire truck on the way to a fire and started to race after it. She soon lost track of where she was running and how long she had been at it. When she stopped running because she lost sight of the truck, she looked around to find she had also traveled to a place she was not familiar with and it was starting to get late. The sun was setting and it was getting dark and it suddenly dawned on her; "I'm lost!" She became afraid and started to scream like she had never screamed before. Soon a policeman found her and was able to take her home. That home never looked so good to her as it did that day.

While Nathan was spending so much time studying and praying with his sons, he missed what was slowly happening to Annie. Rebecca had grown up very poor in Poland, and there was never enough food and often went hungry as a child. It was just something she never forgot, and because of this, Rebecca was always filling Annie's plate with very large portions of food. In Rebecca's mind, a heavy child was a healthy child. Annie, being a child looking to please her mother, hated to fight with her about anything. Because of this Annie usually pushed herself away from the table stuffed and uncomfortable.

Rebecca always told her to clean her plate because there were starving children in the world. Annie always wondered how cleaning her own plate would help the poor starving children. It made no sense to her. Not until she was much older did she realize that it meant you should be happy you have food to eat when others were starving. Why can't parents ever explain things to kids clearly?

Slowly Annie over time was on her way to becoming a chunky young girl. Adding to the problem was that she never had the proper clothes to wear to help hide her rapidly changing figure. Every night Annie would push herself away from the table stuffed and uncomfortable. By the time she was twelve she was definitely an overweight youngster.

Around this age there are always children that look for something or someone to pick on. It is their way of having fun, and unfortunately Annie became the target for the taunting with names like "fatty" and "baby elephant". It seemed everyone was just having a field day calling her names.

The continuous taunting upset her greatly, and every day when she got home she didn't even stop to say hello to any of her family. She just ran to her room, closed the door, putting her back to it, and cried. If her tormentors had used physical force, they could not have been more hurtful. Not only did the kids taunt her; the adults were always saying what a beautiful face she had. From which she inferred that the rest of her body was ugly. Annie had been brought up with the rule: "If you can't say something nice say nothing at all." She wondered why everyone else couldn't follow the same rule. Since her parents' friends did not want to be rude and ignore her altogether, why couldn't they remark on the fact that she was very, very smart? Shouldn't that count for something nice to say?

One day, when she was thirteen and in junior high school, she decided to put an end to the torment once and for all, When she got home from school she went straight to her room and walked up to the mirror and for the first time in her life took a real hard look at herself. What she saw was a fat and ugly girl with a face that would be beautiful if it were only thinner. She felt truly ashamed, and asked herself, "When did all this happen to me?" Oh, how she wished to God that she was skinny again. She was now determined to lose weight and do it as fast as she could. The problem was that when Annie made up her mind to do something, she did it to the extreme, and in this case she decided that she would not just change her eating habits; she would stop eating altogether!

Her plan was just to play with her food and spread it around on her plate. Whenever her mother turned her back Annie would throw some of her food out the window into the courtyard. The alley cats and stray dogs were leaving no trace of what Annie was doing. Her father and brothers were too busy talking about Shul, sports, work, and anything else that did not require them to pay attention to Annie. It was not that they didn't love her. It was just the way things were. Men spoke to men and women spoke to women, so it was easy for Annie to continue to get rid of her food without anyone questioning her. She figured why tell the family what she was doing and why she was doing it? They would never understand anyway.

This routine went on month after month and Annie began to see the changes in her body weight and at first she was very happy. But eventurally she became very pale, had no energy and her hair started to thin and fall out, and since she was no longer feeding her body what it needed, she could not fight off infection and she came down with a severe case of pneumonia. Her mother got worried when Annie could not get up to go to school. She had stayed home with a temperature and a bad cough for three days now. Chicken soup and tea were not helping so Dr. Bernstein was called to come to the house as Annie could not even lift her head up off the pillow. In the good old days doctors still made house calls so patients were not exposed to the ills of others. You only went into the doctor's office for shots and checkups, never if you were sick with an illness that could spread to others. What a concept! The doctor blamed her condition on malnutrition and told Rebecca she must give Annie juices and cereals and red meat. If she made sure her daughter did as she was told she should have a full recovery.

Rebecca was shocked and when Annie finally told her why she had stopped eating. Rebecca got very angry with her, and she got angry with herself as well because she never caught on to what her daughter was doing. From then on Rebecca never turned her back on her daughter again and made sure she ate everything she was supposed to.

Annie could now control what she ate and how much. She ate healthy foods in small portions as she was determined to work hard at still losing weight but not at the cost of her health. She understood it was not good if she became skinny and died. That was not what she wanted. Annie got better slowly and was soon able to go back to school, and when she did everyone noticed all the weight she had lost. They also noticed that she had lost some of her sparkle and was not the happy-go-lucky person she had once been. Slowly even that came back and then kids were no longer picking on her and teasing her and they seemed to look at her in a different way, and she liked it.

She also began to be aware that Nathan and Rebecca were bickering constantly and that Rebecca was always nagging him. It made the apartment a place of unhappiness. The reason Rebecca nagged so much was that Nathan was always engrossed in playing cards with his sons, reading or praying and so paid little attention to her.

Annie always loved to hear adults talk about what life had been like in "the old country" and how happy they were to be able to live in America. Sometimes she heard someone crying over news that someone they had left behind in "the old country" had died. She knew that meant they would never get to see a parent, grandparent, or family member again. She felt herself very fortunate not to have had to live through the hunger, fear, and pogroms that others had to endure. It was just something that belonged to another generation or another world. She was lucky never to have experienced such times.

As this beautiful child grew up, she lived through the good times and bad. Nathan and Rebecca tried to save money for a rainy day. She learned at an early age that money was not something you spent on silly things. As a young child, subjects regarding money did not interest or bother Annie in the least. She knew no different and believed that everyone lived in the same way. It never occurred to her, as a child, that things could be different in other households.

ROSE

In 1920 Annie entered high school. She was fourteen and she was a new person. She had more confidence and a new figure. She wanted to leave "Annie" behind with all her problems and memories. She told her parents she wanted a new start and a new name. Annie went on to tell her parents that she now had a "Rosie" outlook, so she wanted to take the name Rose. Rebecca and Nathan agreed it was a great name for her and gave her their blessing. It was also about this time that she began to notice boys. Often her brothers would bring home friends and all of a sudden, they all seemed to notice their sister was no longer a baby. Being the over-protective brothers they were they decided never to let her go out alone. They were not about to entertain the thought that Rose may be getting to the age where she would think about dating.

Because Nathan and Rebecca had a rule, that they wanted Rose to come straight home after school, Rose missed out on being able to hang out with other boys and girls. This led to her not developing any close "friends." Because of this, she did not have someone to talk with about boys or the newest movie heart throb, or the changes that she was feeling in her body. One day at school Rose got stomach cramps like she never had before and her back was also hurting her terribly. Later that morning, she thought she felt something wet in her panties and was frightened. She excused herself from class, and went to the bathroom. She pulled down her underpants and saw blood. She thought to herself, "Why am I bleeding? I never hurt myself." She was so scared that she was going to die of some dreaded disease.

Even though she was embarrassed, she went straight to the school nurse. It was left up to the nurse to explain what was happening. The nurse had to explain such matters all the time, because there was no sex education in schools in those days and mothers rarely told their daughters what to expect as their bodies changed. This was the way Rosie learned about menstruation, how to keep herself clean and what to expect.

When she got home after school that day Rose told her mother what had happened. Without taking a thought or breath, Rebecca slapped Rose right across the face. This was the first time Rose had ever been struck by either of her parents and she was shocked and started to cry. Rose said, "I am so sorry, Mama. Did I do something wrong? I didn't mean to bleed in my panties, but I had no control over it." Rebecca then took her daughter into her arms and said, "You have done nothing wrong, my daughter." Then she explained that it was an old Jewish custom that the first time a young girl gets her menstrual period the mother must smack her daughter across the cheek to bring the blood back up to her face where it belonged. Rose made a promise to herself then and there. "If I am ever blessed with a daughter, I will tell her about the changes that will take place in her teen years before they happen. And I will not slap her across the cheek without saying something about it first."

WHEN HARRY MET ROSE

On a summer day, in late 1921 Rose met Harry by Chance for the first time. Rose was only fifteen and Harry was twenty-six. Rose was walking to the butcher shop to pick up a chicken so her mother could make dinner. She was on Broadway in Brooklyn when she heard the train pull to a stop in the elevated train station over the butcher shop. She loved to watch the passengers step off the train onto the platform and descend the stairs, so she stopped and looked up. On this particular day she noticed mostly soldiers in uniform, and imagined that they were just returning home from their assignments overseas. As Rose looked at the different people, she saw one person she could not help but stare at intently. For some strange reason she could not pull her vision away from the solider coming toward her. Rose always felt she would meet her special someone in an unconventional way, and this soldier looked to be out of place because he was older than most of the boys in uniform. Most of the soldiers she saw were still in their teens or early twenties, but this man looked to be at least thirty. He was carrying his large green duffel bag on his shoulder and she thought he was the most handsome man she had ever seen. Her heart started to race, and she asked herself, "Could this one be my Prince Charming?" All the other people descending the steps seemed to disappear and he was the only one she could see. At the same time, as Rose was looking at this stunning man, the stunning man also had his eyes fixed on her. He smiled, and Rose blushed and he could not help but to keep on smiling back at her as he descended the final few stairs and he thought to himself, "I've never seen a more perfect girl in all my life." What he saw was a beautiful face framed by long black hair, big brown eyes, and porcelain skin with a pink glow to it. He also saw she had a contagious smile and he thought: "I wonder how old she is."

Rose turned her head away and stopped looking at this strange man and continued to walk. If she did not continue to walk, she felt her heart would break open from beating so hard and fast. As she turned and walked away she tried to calm herself down. She had to tell herself to take slow deep breaths. All of a sudden she felt the presence of another person walking along side of her. Rose kept walking but turned slightly to see who it was. It startled her to see it was the soldier. After a moment he said, "Hi, my name is Harry Rubin. I've just spent the last eight years in the Army." As he spoke, Rose gave him a close once-over. She noticed that he had both his arms and legs, and his face was not scarred. She thought, "Wow, he had gotten through the war untouched!" Harry said, "It is my first time back home in a long time, and many things seem to have changed around here. I am trying to find my way to an apartment on Siegel Street. Do you think you might be able to help me?" Rose was speechless, but for some reason she felt safe and not threatened. He was just asking directions and Rose thought not to help a soldier who had just returned from war would be a *shanda* (a bad thing). Rose thought that they were, after all, in a very public place with many people moving all around them, although neither one of them seemed to notice that they were not alone. She stopped walking and just looked up into his eyes, and mustered the nerve to answer him back "Hi, my name is Rose." She then thought to herself, "What am I doing talking to a complete stranger? If someone saw us and told my family, what would they think of me?"

It was 1922 and the war had ended four years earlier, and it was still not acceptable for a young lady to speak to a gentleman that she had not been properly introduced to let alone be seen with. This type of chance meeting was becoming more acceptable, but was not readily accepted yet, especially in the Orthodox community. Harry smiled his most charming smile and continued the conversation. "I'm really happy to be back home. I have missed my family and can't wait to have a real home-cooked meal, sleep in a real bed, and take a hot bath." Harry did not know why he was telling this complete stranger all about his wishes; he only knew that he did not want to see her walk away from him. So he continued speaking. At one point he grabbed onto her arm to keep her from being knocked over by a passing man. Rose had not yet done anything but tell him her name, and she just stood there looking at him. All Rose kept thinking was how very handsome he was and with a name like Harry Rubin, he would have to be Jewish. This was a good thing as she was already in love.

Harry had a big bright smile, blue eyes, a wonderful suntan and being in uniform did not hurt the look of the entire package. When she smiled slightly at him Harry felt a little more confident and told her he was twenty-six and had served most of the time in Panama. By now, they had started walking again and Harry was doing all the talking. But he didn't care; he just wanted to be near her for as long as he could. He told her he had been very sick at the end of the war and could not go back to the front lines, so he had just spent the last four years serving as an Army recruiter in Georgia. Rose turned onto Bushwick Avenue. "Oh," she said, "I'm so sorry. I just kept walking toward my home and never told you how to get to yours. You have to walk back to the train station which is on Broadway, and make a left not a right and then you will come to Siegel Street. He said, "Thanks for your help. Do you think I could call on you some time? I don't know anyone around here and I could use a friend to show me around. I have been gone so long, I really don't know who will be able to take the time to help me."

Rose knew her parents would not want her roaming around with a much older man. Plus she would have to deal with her four brothers as well. She decided that she would deal with the fallout later, so she threw caution to the wind and told Harry she would meet him the next day at the train station at half past three in the afternoon.

Harry walked back toward home. He of course knew the way. He just asked directions as a way of trying to speak a little longer to Rose. He was a worldly solider who had lived through horrors no man should and along the way had many "adventures. Harry asked himself why this one girl was pulling so strongly at his heart?

Rose had not told Harry much about herself on their short walk to her front stoop. Once Harry left, Rose ran back to the butcher shop to pick up the chicken her mother wanted, then ran all the way back home. When she got into the apartment, her cheeks were flushed and she was out of breath. Her brother Frank was in the living room reading a book. As she entered, he looked up and said, "Are you ok? Your face is very red."

As Frank looked at her, he noticed for the first time that Annie his baby sister was no longer a baby. She was growing into a very beautiful young lady. Annie wondered what he would think if he knew she had just met the perfect stranger and that she was just floating on air. Annie was dying to tell someone about the young man she had just met. But she thought twice about telling anyone about it, because she knew it was crazy. How could anyone fall in love so fast and how can fate put someone in the right place at the right time and change a person's life so completely? Every thought she had on her mind was of Harry. She had to find a way to tell him that she was still in high school, that she had never been kissed by a boy or been out on a date. Rose knew that her family was over-protective and she did not know how they would react if she were found out.

Little did Rose know that just a few short blocks away Harry was thinking of her. He was thinking things like "I can't believe I just met this beautiful woman and I don't even know her last name." He had a fitful night sleep and his dreams were not of his hard life in Panama but of the girl he had met that day. Harry thought, "She was just as beautiful as the most delicate Rose I have ever seen." Harry's instinct for people had kept out of trouble many times. He knew who would stand by his side in a fight and who he would never turn his back on. He somehow knew that this girl was so different from any girl he had ever met before.

Having been in the Army for so many years he had met many young girls, but no one had struck him like this one had. He knew she must have been sheltered all her life and from the way she was dressed, covered from head to toe, he guessed she came from a religious family. Harry thought to himself, "Maybe I should not see her again. Maybe I won't be able to live up to her expectations. I have lived through and seen so much in my life that it would not be fair to burden such a delicate flower with my needs."

Harry spent his first day home helping his mother. He went with her down to the pushcarts where the vendors were trying to sell their wares. They bought food, some civilian clothing for Harry, and anything else she wanted. Harry tried to make up for not being around when the family came over from Russia. All the time he was out with his mother, all Harry could think about was Rose and the impact she had made on him.

Rose tossed and turned the whole night thinking about Harry. For some reason she just had the feeling that this strange man would change her whole life. She had had no experience with boys let alone men and Harry was definitely a man. There was no doubt about that. The strange feeling she felt was the awareness of her body. Rose wished she was even thinner than she was, and she just knew that she could not wait to see him again. Rose wished that she had someone she could talk to and confide in, but she didn't. She awoke early the next morning, before anyone else in the apartment. She took her bath and washed herself and her hair as she normally did before school. She didn't have to curl her hair like so many other girls did, because her hair fell so beautifully into curls on its own. She powdered herself and searched her closet for something special to wear. She had nothing except a white blouse and black skirt, which was her holiday outfit. After she put on her outfit, she told her parents that she was meeting some friends at the library after school to study. She did this so they would not be concerned when she did not come straight home from school as usual.

Rose had saved $2.29 as her emergency money just in case something important came up. She left the house and on the way to school she went to the local drugstore. There she bought a bottle of cologne, stockings, and a flower for her hair. She went into a public bathroom and finished her dressing. She looked into the mirror and wished she were prettier. Rose had to spend the whole day in school, and knew concentrating would be hard for the first time in her life. Some of the kids she went to school with told her she looked very nice and asked her where she was going. "No place special, I just wanted a change." Rose liked that some of her friends noticed that she looked good. Rose kept thinking to herself "I only hope Harry notices how pretty I feel." After school, (the longest school day of her life) Rose headed straight to the train station. She got there with fifteen minutes to spare before Harry was suppose to arrive.

There was a bench right near the station, so Rose sat down to wait. She turned toward the sun hoping the few minutes she had to wait would put some color in her face. While she sat there, she was daydreaming about the life Harry must have led over the many years in the Army. She also wondered why he had even stopped to speak to her. Before she knew it, Harry was there and sat down right next to her. He said, "Hi, I hope you haven't been waiting long?" Rose replied "No, I just got here myself." Harry asked "Shall we take a little walk?" "Sure, there is a park not too far from here," Rose replied.

So they walked and talked and to Rose everything in the world was beautiful. She felt a happiness she had never felt before. He touched her arm to keep her from tripping and Rose felt a warm thrill run through her body which she had never before experienced and she felt her cheeks flush. Harry had the same feelings. *How ridiculous* he thought. *I have never felt this way before. Could there really be such a thing as love at first sight?* They walked and talked for over an hour. They sat on a park bench and continued talking, taking no heed of the things going on around them or of the day slipping away. Harry did most of the talking, telling Rose about what it was like growing up in Russia, the pogroms, his flight to freedom, joining the army, and anything else he could think of. He was just afraid if he stopped talking they would have to put an end to the day.

Rose told him that she and her brothers were born in America, but she knew what life had been like for her parents before they got married and were able to come over on the ship to the United States. They laughed about the possibility that Harry and her parents may have all been on the same ship. As the sun was setting Harry walked Rose back to her building. Before he could think about what he was, doing Harry leaned toward Rose and gave her a kiss right smack on her lips! Rose was astounded, but after the shock began to wear off, she got her voice back and agreed to meet Harry at the same spot the next day. As he turned to walk away, Rose brought her fingers tips to her lips and then placed her fingers on his lips. She was so excited that she was almost sixteen and now she had been kissed and by a man not a boy.

As Harry walked away, he thought to himself; "It's incredible. I have been all over the world and lived to come back home and the first day back I meet the woman of my dreams." He knew he just had to get to know her and the sooner the better. Harry had never given thought to getting married and having kids. Harry loved kids. He wondered how old Rose really was, and he was hoping she was at least eighteen and free to marry him. Little did he know that she had turned fifteen just six months ago. Harry knew he would need her parents' permission before she could marry. Would they let her? It was not natural for girls in America to marry as young as they did in Europe.

Harry got up early the next morning to start looking for a job. As insane as it may seem, he knew he wanted to ask Rose to marry him. Everywhere Harry tried to apply for a job, he heard the same thing over and over again. "Come back next week. Maybe I'll have something for you then." By this time, it was late in the afternoon and time for him to meet Rose and he still had no job. There were jobs out there but they paid so little it would have been ok when he was a kid right off the boat, but he had served his country in the Army for ten years. With all his sacrifice and experience the only jobs he could get were jobs that paid five dollars a week. He knew he could not support Rose and himself on such a low wage.

While killing some time before he had to meet Rose, Harry walked into a local candy store and ran into his old friend Fat Artie. Harry met and became close friends with Fat Artie in 1911, when he was delivering mattresses through the crowded streets of Brooklyn. Artie was just standing there and when he saw Harry, he walked up to him and gave him such a big tight bear hug Harry thought his ribs were going to crack. Once he was let go and could catch his breath, he began talking about the old days and what he been doing since the last time he and Artie saw each other. Harry explained he joined the Army in 1912 and spent eight years in Panama and two years as a recruiter in New York City. He told Artie that he was recently honorably discharged and could not find a job that paid a decent wage.

After talking for a short time, Artie offered Harry a job. Everyone knew that with the start of Prohibition on January 16, 1920 and the passage of the Eighteenth Amendment to the United States Constitution the government was not allowing the manufacture, transportation, or sale of alcoholic beverages in the United States. Artie told Harry that if you tell people that they can't have something, they will find a way to get it. Artie explained he had some friends who were setting up stills in their basements or sheds and selling it to speakeasies and other underground drinking establishments. He emphasized that large quantities of alcohol were being smuggled into the States from Canada.

He said that organized crime had taken over most of the importing and making of alcohol and anyone who tried to horn in on their operation was dealt with harshly, and he was looking for people who would not turn tail and run if things got tough (as they often did), someone who could lead men, and who would not be afraid to use a gun. The job involved driving a truck, making deliveries of bootleg alcohol for the racketeers, and making sure the truck and shipment were not high jacked. It was a dangerous job but Harry knew he could make a great deal of money. Artie said he would make a call and get him started. Harry told Artie that he would have to think about it and would meet him back in the candy store in three days with his answer. As Harry thought about the consequences of taking the job, he worried how his father, the Cantor, would react to him being a bootlegger. Harry was also smart enough to know that without a proper education he was not going to get a good legitimate job. He also knew there was danger in doing the job that Fat

Artie had proposed. He figured out that he might get shot or arrested. He also realized that he would not be content with a five-dollar a week job, which was the going rate for a man like him with no formal education.

While Harry was thinking about the offer, Fat Artie was speaking to his friends about Harry. He told them that Harry had spent ten years in the Army, knew his way around guns and could handle himself in a crisis. He also knew that Harry wanted to earn good money and that five hundred dollars a week would be something Harry could not walk away from. After listening to Artie the mob bosses were very interested in Harry and wanted him working for them, not the competition.

Again Rose did not sleep well. She had this nervous feeling that was new to her. She had no one to talk to. She was sure she had met the man she would marry and knew in her heart of hearts there could never be another. Rose already had their lives planned out. They would own a house in the country and would have three children and be happy for the rest of their lives.

Rose met Harry the next day at the bottom of the steps leading to the elevated train platform which they called their steps. They both arrived at the same time and before they knew what was happening they flew into each other's arms and were passionately kissing right there out in public This was in plain view of where everyone was passing by and neither one seemed to care. Harry held on to Rose and would not let her go.

They both knew this was something special, so Harry looked into Rose's dark eyes and said; "Rose will you marry me and be my wife?" Once Rose caught her breath she threw her arms around his neck and said: "Oh yes, Harry, I will marry you and be your wife."   Harry and Rose decided to go to Rose's home and introduce Harry to her family. When they arrived at the Cohen's apartment, Rose introduced Harry to her parents. As was customary Rebecca offered everyone a glass of tea. While drinking his tea, Harry asked Nathan for his permission to marry Rose. At first Nathan and Rebecca were shocked and concerned because Rose was only fifteen and would not be sixteen until December, which was six months away. They also were concerned because they did not know where she had even met this man, and they were uneasy about him because of his forwardness. Leib and Rebecca wanted to know more about Harry and his background so they began asking him many personal questions. After talking with him for about an hour they started to feel better about him. They were impressed that he was the son of a Cantor, so they knew that he came from a good devout home.

Harry briefly recounted his long journey to escape from Russia and how he made it to Brooklyn. He also told them about his three-month tour of Europe and his experiences in the Army. He told them how he had saved all his money and sent it back home to bring his family to America. Rose took that moment to remind her parents that when they married, Rebecca had only been 16. Nathan saw a man not afraid to stand up for his country and one who sacrificed to bring his family to safety. Harry assured her parents and wary brothers that he loved Rose and would always take care of her. Nathan gave the marriage proposal his blessing and with great joy in their hearts the happy couple left to go over to the home of Harry's parents.

Both Harry and Rose thought the visit with Harry's parents would be much easier, but Cantor Rabinowitz and Fanny were just as shocked to meet Rose as her parents were to meet Harry. Leib and Fannie had never before heard Harry mention Rose. Many questions were running through their minds "Where did she come from? How long have they know each other? Was she even Jewish?" Fannie had everyone sit down at the kitchen table and fixed them each of them a glass of tea and tried to get some answers. In the end Fanny and Lieb were happy, specially with the fact that Rose came from a good religious home. This was more than they expected from their wayward son. Their hope was that maybe now he would settle down and be a family man.

Fanny showed Rose around the apartment and told her that when they got married they could use their back bedroom for as long as they needed. Rose thanked Fanny and they hugged and kissed. Both women were feeling good about each other. From the first moment Rose met Harry's parents she immediately loved them and felt a warmth and friendliness she had never felt from strangers before. Rose realized these lovely people would be her new family and Rose felt good about it. She just knew she and Harry would have a perfect life together.

That day Lieb, Fanny, Harry and Rose talked for a long time about the wedding arrangements. Looking at the calendar they figured out there was a problem. During the Spring time there were many Jewish holidays and only a few days in the next two months that Jewish law would allow weddings to be performed. Both Harry and Rose did not want to wait. So they had a choice to make. They had either to get married within the following two weeks or to wait another seven weeks until after the Jewish holidays ended. The decision Harry and Rose made was simple, As they wanted to get married a soon as possible, the wedding was set to take place in two weeks on June 22, 1922, just before the holidays. It seemed quite fast, they hardly knew each other, but everyone knew it had to be then.

The next day Harry returned to the candy store at the time agreed upon with Fat Artie, who arrived a few minutes late. When he asked Harry what he had decided about the job, Harry told him that he was to be married soon, and was having a problem finding a good job that would support him and his soon-to-be-wife. So Harry accepted the job offer and told Artie he would do his best. Artie was thrilled and told Harry he had made the right choice and he would contact him about when and where he would start.

On June 22, 1922, two weeks and three days after Harry and Rose first met at their subway steps, they were married. The wedding ceremony was a traditional Orthodox ceremony conducted by Harry's father, Cantor Lieb Rabiniowitz in his own apartment. It was a small apartment, so only immediate family members were invited. Harry's sister Leah stood up as her maid of honor, and Harry's brother Jack was best man. Cantor Rabinowitz thought he had never seen a more beautiful bride. To have gone through what they had all suffered and be able to be part of this wonderful day was more than he could have ever wished for. He only prayed that Rose would be strong enough to handle his son. The Cantor knew his son well and knew in his heart that it would not be an easy road for his new daughter to travel, and she was so young. The four Chuppah (Jewish wedding canopy) poles were held by Rose's four brothers -- Frank, Simon, Jack, and Emil (Jerry) and the canopy was made from the Tallit that had belonged to one of Harry's great grandfathers. When Harry broke the glass (a real glass, not a light bulb as is used by many people today) the room erupted in shouts of 'MAZEL TOV" (which means good luck).

By the time the wedding took place Harry had already started working for his friend Fat Artie and had made quite a few runs to both Coney Island and Long Island. It was exciting for him to be in the middle of the action. He was making $500 dollars a week which was a hundred times what most men were making at a regular jobs. When Harry told Fat Artie about his wedding plans, he offered Harry the use of his car. He suggested Harry take Rose to a beautiful place in the Catskill Mountains in upstate New York. It was a place called the Laurel Hotel, and he could take his new bride on a "honeymoon" (also not something common in those days). To be able to go to a "vacation" spot where you could keep the Jewish dietary laws was a blessing for many and would become a big business in the Catskills in later years. It was more than Harry could have asked for, but with more money in his pocket than he had ever dreamed of he wanted to show Rose a good time.

After the wedding was over and all the well wishers had left, Harry took Rose outside to show her the car he had borrowed and told her of his plans for a honeymoon. All Rose could do was gasp and start to cry with happiness and joy. She had never been in a car before, but she never felt afraid. She had complete trust in her new husband. After all at fifteen she was Mrs. Harry Rubin and she felt the world was hers and she knew that Harry would always be there to protect her.

They drove for five hours to get to the Catskills and Harry sang songs to her all the way. It was his way of trying to keep her at ease. Rose had never before heard most of the songs he was singing and asked him to sing them over and over. Harry had pulled off the road a few times along the way just so he could kiss her. Rose could feel Harry tenderly holding his breath, hoping he would not scare her. While driving, Harry would often reach for her hand to squeeze it and to tell her how much he loved her. That plus the singing made the time fly by.

When she got out of the car, Rose found herself in front of the biggest most beautiful hotel she had ever seen. It had a big lake right out back, and the scenery was breathtaking. Rose thought to herself that this was quite an adventure, but she was more than a little frightened. Her mother had not told her what to expect when she had gotten her period, and she had also not told her what to expect on her wedding night. At that time sex education was not taught in the public schools, as it is today, plus there was no talk about sex in the movies, or on the radio. Today talk of sex is everywhere. It is prominent on television, movies, and the internet. This has prepared girls for sexual relations prematurely. By the time they are ten, there is usually nothing more to learn. Most girls and boys are not even virgins when they marry today. In Rose's case she hardly knew this man that was now her husband, and she would soon be asked to consummate the marriage. Rebecca had only told Rose the vaguest of facts the morning of her wedding day. She told Rose that sex was an obligation women had to perform in order to make babies and keep their husbands happy.

Grandfather, Cantor Leib.

Harry, in the United States Army, aged 18.

Lieb and the congregation.

Harry's military orders to Panama.

My other grandfather, Nathan, and Grandma Rebecca.

Brother Charlie, aged 7, a pianist since 4yrs. Old.

Brothers Jackie and Charlie, 1948.

Harry and Rose in Laurelton, New York, 1946.

Irene, aged 19—an Armed Forces Sweetheart.

Harry, 1940s, always dapper.

Sister Marion, 1948, a Barbizon model.

Son Richard's Bar Mitzvah, 1961.

Irene and Harry, 1966.

Irene and best friend, Pearl, 1967.

Irene and Arnie, 1967.

Irene and Henry Winkler and the wonderful
Sam Silverstein, Irene's film partner.

Irene and Eddie Fisher. Eat your hearts
out, Debbie and Elizabeth.

Irene, first woman president of the cinema,
radio, and TV unit of the Bnai Brith.

The Levy clan, 1980.

Irene and Arnie

Daughter Janis' high school graduation, 1983.

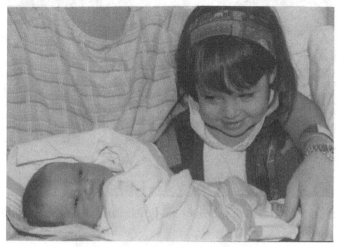

Granddaughters Mariel and Aliya saying
hi to each other for the first time.

The Levy Clan on the occasion of
Irene's 80th birthday, 2004.

Jennifer, with Irene's daughters, Janis, Linda, Andrea, 2006.

Mariel and Aliya, 2006, great friends.

ELLIS ISLAND
— 1892–1992 —

The Statue of Liberty-Ellis Island Foundation, Inc.

proudly presents this

Official Certificate of Registration

in

THE AMERICAN IMMIGRANT WALL OF HONOR

to officially certify that

Harry Rubin

who came to America from

Russia

is among those courageous men and women who came to this country in search of personal freedom, economic opportunity and a future of hope for their families.

Lee A. Iacocca
The Statue of Liberty-Ellis Island
Foundation, Inc.

LIBERTY
1886-1986

Harry, remembered at Ellis Island.

Granddaughters Samantha, Jessica, and Juliette. 2013 the "Belles of Florida…"

Andrea, 2013.

Irene and Charlie at Irene's 90th, 2014.

Grandson, Danny, with Anna Carla, and baby
Sidonia, Irene's first great great-grandchild

Irene at 91, the new 55...

522 Shore Road, Long Beach, NY

Lou and Ruth, left us within a month of each other.

PART TWO

PART TWO

MY MOTHER

TREYF
1922

Three months after Harry met Rose they
got married. They moved into an apartment
in a building four doors away from Lieb and
Fanny in Brooklyn. Rose came from a very
religious home, but Harry was not religious
at all. One day Rose visited her parents who
lived one mile away. When she came home
and walked to her apartment door, she smelled
something strange. When she opened the door,
she found Harry and three of his Army friends
frying bacon. She ran out crying and ran to
Lieb's and Fanny's apartment down the block.
She knocked at the door and when Lieb let
her in, she was hysterical. She described to
him what had happened.

Lieb put his hand on her head and said,
"Daughter, if you love my son, forget about
the food."

For a religious man to say this was not easy.
But he knew his son.

FROM BROOKLYN TO LONG ISLAND
1926

Hard work. Harry had to deliver the booze
at night to avoid trouble, getting caught by
the police or being knocked off by other
bootleggers. There were many people in the
same business who would have liked to get
rid of Harry. He slept during the day. Rose
had to be quiet and keep little Irene quiet
which was almost impossible. They hardly
saw each other. He sorely missed his wife
and baby daughter but he was making big money
and was making big plans how to spend it.
He managed to get to Long Island on one
off day and see the beautiful town of
Laurelton. He saw a house he would love
to buy and found he could afford it. Two years
after Irene was born, Louis was born, a boy
they named after Harry's father, Lieb.

One day Harry said to Rose, "I'm taking the
day off. My mother will watch the children. You
and I are going for a ride to Long Island." Rose
was so happy for the lapse in her regular routine.
It was perfect weather and Rose could not get
over the beauty of Long Island scenery. Harry had
borrowed a car from his friend Arty. He never told
Rose he had been there before. He showed her the
house he liked and wanted to buy. Rose was shocked.
Imagine living in this beautiful place and having a house

with three bedrooms, living room, etc., on a little
hill, peach stucco, a front porch and backyard. What a
difference from living in a small railroad flat in Brooklyn.
It was more than Rose ever dreamed of. He actually bought
the house. They moved in the next week. Everything they
had was hauled by a big truck. Little Irene and Louis now
lived with their parents in Laurelton, Long Island after
two years beautiful Marion was born.

LITTLE CHARLIE

I adored Charlie, who died when
I was ten. It still hurts when I think
about him. He was beautiful with
blond curls and big blue eyes. I
treated him like he was my baby.
He called me Iri. One day my mother
noticed he was coughing. She took
his temperature. It was a hundred
and two. She immediately took him
to our family doctor. When Doctor
Friedland examined him he found
Charlie had a strep throat. He told
us to take him to the hospital. The
nearest one was Jamaica Hospital.
In his room he cried, afraid of being
in a strange place. He kept calling my
name, Iri. There was no penicillin in
those days. I'll never forget the funeral.

We walked over hills and everyone was
crying and screaming. My mother was
held back by her two brothers. And she
wanted to jump into the grave with her
baby. She had a nervous breakdown.
She blamed my father for moving from
Laurelton to Hollis. The house was
sometimes cold. Then she got worse
and my father had to put her in an
institution. Every few months she came
home. It was so hard for my father, watching
the children, me, Louie and Marion, and working.
Little Charlie died on my father's fortieth birthday,
March 4th. The cure in those days was shock treatment.
I sat with my mother while she was getting it. The worst
thing I ever saw. It gave the paitient convulsions. She
seemed much better after that. The doctor mentioned
to my father that perhaps having more children would
help her forget. She had a little boy. And they named
him Charlie after Little Charlie. He looked exactly
like Little Charlie with beautiful blond curls and blue
eyes. Then she had another son, named Jack. Every
once in a while she had to go back into the hospital.
It was a terrible thing for the kids and my father.

ONE FRIEND

Because Rose was so young when she married
Harry, she had no experience with housekeeping.

When she had children and she had to make baby
food, she found it very difficult. She never had time
to socialize or make friends. After I married and Rose
met my mother-in-law, Helen, they became fast
friends. Helen had many friends, but she was Rose's
only friend. In later years I saw and appreciated the
fact that Helen was so good to my
mother.

GLORIA DEHAVEN

One day I called my Mom and said,
"Could you babysit for us tonight.
We were just given two tickets for
a Broadway show."

She said, "I can't. Because I watch this
program every afternoon on tv."

It seems this beautiful blond actress
Gloria DeHaven, had a talk show
and apparently my mother answered
a question and won three silver bowls.

I explained she could watch at our house
and she finally agreed.

My husband and I went to New York early
and went to dinner and then to the show. As we
walked into the lobby, who was there but Gloria
DeHaven.

I went over to her and explained that I almost
missed the show because of her.

I said, "My mother didn't want to miss your show so she didn't want to babysit for us but I talked her into it. Her name is Mrs. Rubin. R-U-B-I-N."

She remembered my mother and then I got a bright idea.

I saw a phone in the lobby and asked her if it was all right if I called my mother.

She said yes.

I said to my mom, "Guess who I just met. And she is going to say hello to you."

My mom was so thrilled and never forgot that call.

My husband and I laughed all the way home.

ALWAYS AND ALWAYS
1975

My Mom Rose lived with me for seven years after my father died. I often played the piano. My mother loved to sing and learned all the songs. Her favorite was *Always and Always.*

Then one day she had a stroke and could no longer talk, so I arranged a place for her in the Hannah Komonoff Pavilion next to the Long Beach Hospital. Otherwise she would have been alone all day, as I had to go to work and had to leave early in the morning and not return until evening. In those days, 1975, the nursing home was beautiful with lots of caring nurses.

The following year my brother Lou and his wife
Ruth, who lived in Babylon, invited the family for
Thanksgiving dinner.

We picked up my mother and her wheelchair.

After a delicious turkey dinner my sister-in-law
sat down and played our favorite songs, one after
another, until she played *Always and Always*.

Though my mother had not talked in a year,
all of a sudden she started to sing. The rest
of us fell silent. She sang the whole song, and
we all stared at her in amazement.

After that she never talked or sang again.

I will always remember the song *Always and
Always*.

A NEW OUTFIT
1974 to 1979

One day Rose complained that she did not
feel well. I took her to the hospital because
her blood pressure was very high. After tests
it was determined that she was being over-medicated.
She spent a whole month in the hospital. The social
worker told my husband Arnie and me that Rose should
go to a nursing home for a while to recover. We brought
her to a very fancy place in Roslyn. The second day she was
there a big walnut door knocked her over. So she had to
go back
to the North Shore Hospital.

She had very bad diabetes and one night I walked in I saw a
nurse bringing her a tray. On it was the worst food a diabetic
could eat. I said to her, "What kind of food are you bringing
my mother. You know she's a diabetic. I'm going to report you."

Again the social worker said the best thing for Mom was a nursing home, as she was still weak.

My mother was sixty-eight at the time. We decided to bring
her to the Hannah Kamenoff Pavilion in Long Beach.
We heard it was very good. It was the best four years of
her life. She was always alone at my house. We worked,
the kids went to school, and she was very lonely. But now
there were lots of people, entertainment and speakers.
Every Sunday I brought a friend, Nat Blank, to play the
piano and sing. They made her chief of her floor and gave
her a badge. She had never cared about clothes, but now
she asked me to get her some. She would sit in the garden,
which was situated on Reynolds Channel, and we would
pass her in our boat and wave to her. The last outfit I
bought her was silk pants and a white Chinese blouse. She
loved it. One day she was sitting with a group
when I visited. I told her I was leaving for one week with
Arnie to visit his mother in Florida. She kissed me and
wished me a happy trip. While in Florida I got a call from
my brother Louie. He was crying and told me that Mom
had heart failure and passed away. I was happy that my

brother was with her all night as she adored him. We came back the next day for the funeral. She was seventy-two. I had the funeral director put the silk pants and Chinese blouse on her.

MY FATHER

BELTS

I remember a dark brown belt
with a gold buckle. It belonged
to my father. He never used it on us.
But if we were bad, he took it off and
said, "If you keep it up, I'll use this
on you." That was enough. We were
afraid of that belt. For a little while
we tried to be good.

LAURELTON

Rose never knew that Harry was making
booze in the basement. Every once in a while
strange men came to see him. They always
went to another room to talk. Harry became
very popular in Laurelton. Of course no-one
knew he was a bootlegger. He joined the American
Legion, the temple and went to every meeting
and every affair. Unfortunately, Rose did not accompany
him. She was exhausted from taking care of her
two children and was pregnant with her third.
She also felt unsure of herself when socializing.

So even though Harry invited her, she never
went with him. Harry was making so much money
he bought a beautiful new car. A blue Pierce Arrow.
When he went to visit Fanny in Brooklyn and parked
the car, people came and stared at it. Every Sunday
Harry had a big party at the house. He invited all
his siblings and a few friends. Anyone who needed
money asked Harry. He was very generous.
Rose gave birth again and had another girl named Marion
after Rose's grandmother Miriam. Marion had blond hair
and big blue eyes. As the years passed Harry bought his
children many toys. On Christmas he would tell them
to go to the bedroom and hide their eyes. The corner
candy
store man named Jack would deliver bicycles, baby
carriages, dolls, little tables and chairs, etc. Harry would
call the children out of the bedroom and they would be
thrilled.

As time went by, Rose became more and more
withdrawn. Harry worried about her but didn't know
what to
do. He taught Irene to sing a song at his Sunday parties. She
would stand on the table and sing. "Everythiing is rosy
and the
goose is hanging high. Come on, Harry, buy a drink. The
crowd is getting dry."

IT WAS THE BEST OF TIMES, IT WAS THE WORST OF TIMES
1929 to 1936

When I grew up in Laurelton I had beautiful
clothes. My father made enough money for me
to take piano lessons. My teacher's name was
Mrs. Pigosh. My brother Louie had a wrestling
instructor and finally Rose had a woman named
Laura who came to help with the house and children.
Harry loved cars and driving and we often took trips
to the Catskill Mountains to a hotel owned by a lady
named Mrs. Hoffman. When we moved to Hollis and
Harry bought a bar and grill the bad luck started. The
death of baby Charlie brought extreme sadness to the
family. Harry bought one bar and grill after another and
every one was unsuccessful. Little by little he lost all his
money. Then we went on relief.

ST. PATRICK'S DAY
1946

St. Patrick's Day reminded me I will never forget
the song *When Irish Eyes Are Smiling*.

One night a long time ago before I was
married I went to a Jewish Orthodox wedding
with my family. I can't seem to remember who got
married. What I do remember is this:

At first hors d'oervres and drinks were served.

My father was in the liquor business but could not drink. That night he had one drink. We all sat down in the back row to watch and listen to the wedding ceremony. I sat on one side of my father and my brother Charlie sat on the other. We both noticed my father was sleeping. We tried to wake him but could not. Finally the ceremony ended and it was announced that dinner was being served in the next room. My father was still sleeping. A small man with a long white beard approached us. We explained that my father was asleep. He went to the bar, got a glass of seltzer. He put it under my father's nose. My father moved his head and finally woke up, singing out loud *When Irish Eyes Are Smiling.*

MY CHILDHOOD

TWINS

In 1924 Rose gave birth to twins, a girl and a
boy. Perhaps because Rose had the
twins at home with a midwife and
not in a hospital with a doctor,
one of the twins, the boy, who weighed
only two pounds, did not survive.
    I am the other twin, the one who survived.
People who knew them in those early years
have said that I became Harry's and Rose's
whole life. They never left me alone. If they
went to the movies, they brought me with them.
They named me Irene after Harry's sister Ida.
I remember Rose as a very good mother.
I was told she nursed me for many months
before feeding me ordinary food.

EDUCATION
1932

When I was eight years old, we went
to the country. We went out on a raft
with a bunch of kids. I couldn't swim.
We were laughing and kidding around.
All of a sudden one of the boys thought

it was very funny to throw me off the
raft. It was a miracle that I started to
move my arms and swim. It was that or
drown.

MISCHIEF

All by myself at the age of eleven I took
a bus from Laurelton to the Broadway EL
and then a train to Williamsburg, Brooklyn,
to see my Grandma Fanny. My cousin Marty,
also eleven, also alone, also took public transport,
but from Staten Island, and met me at my Grandma's.

We played a game in the living room and then
got bored.

We saw a small mirror on the end table and
got an idea. We would shine it on the bald head
of the delicatessen man across the street.

He was working and felt something strange.
He kept rubbing his head and looking up.

He finally saw!

He called the police.

A policeman knocked at the door and my
Grandma answered.

"Not my ainelka (*grandchildren*). My ainelka
wouldn't do that."

We were hiding under the bed.

My Grandma fed the policeman home-made

apple strudel and hot tea.

And then he left.

WORDS

One lovely Spring morning my father said, "Let's take a ride
to see my old Army friend who lives in Freeport."

We all agreed that would be a good idea.

We went straight on Merrick Road. We were riding along in Lynbrook when my father passed a red light.
In one minute a policeman blew a whistle and stopped us.

He wrote a ticket.

I was sitting in the back seat.

Some nerve writing a ticket for my Daddy.

I stood up. I was five. I reached over, pulled the ticket out of
the policeman's hand, ripped it up, then threw it in his face.
I started to call him every dirty word I knew.

He looked at me, then wrote my father a ticket. It was way more than the original ticket.

My father never hit me, not even this time, but he did scream at me.

To this day I never use a dirty word.

TONSILS
1929

How far back can you remember?
I remember when I was five years old.
I was told the doctor was coming.
I pulled the belt off my bathrobe
and tied it across the crib. I hated
the doctor. All of a sudden he was there.
I even remember his name. His name was
Doctor Gitlin. To my horror he reached in
and got me. I know I was screaming. He
took me and put me on the kitchen table.
I was surprised to see my younger brother
and sister there also screaming. I suppose
he gave us a sedative because suddenly
we were quiet.

Then he removed our tonsils. How come
we all needed our tonsils out at once. Was
it cheaper? Did we all need our tonsils out?
When I look back I wonder if Doctor Gitlin
gave tonsil operations cheap. He probably
told my parents, "I can do it for you wholesale."

DISASTER

I was very sad about the Holocaust,
John Kennedy's death, the Titanic,
and Pearl Harbor, but I had a disaster

in my family.

I was only ten when my baby brother, Charlie, died in the hospital. A beautiful sweet child. We adored him. He got a strep throat and there was no penicillin. He called me Irie. I still remember this like it was yesterday. I remember the cemetery. My mother was screaming. She had a nervous breakdown. And the whole family suffered for a long time. He died on March 4th, my father's fortieth birthday.

And years later my father died on Charlie's birthday, July 16th.

MY MARRIAGE

HOW I MET MY HUSBAND

In high school I was talking to a girl
sitting in back of me. She raved about
an Arnie that she saw every Saturday
night. On the train the next day I met another
friend who also raved about an Arnie,
an Arnie she saw every *Friday* night. When I heard
this I suspected they both had the same boyfriend.
He took one girl out on Friday nights and the other on
Saturday
nights.

About this time a guy in high school, a guy called
Dickie,
asked me for a date. He took me to a drive-in on Sunrise
Highway. He put his arm around me and tried to kiss me.
I said no. He took me home. Apparently he found someone
who would kiss him and decided to ask his friend Arnie
if they could go out on Arnie's father's boat on Saturday
night. Arnie said I don't have a date. His Saturday night
date
had a family affair. So Dickie suggested me. He said to
Arnie, "She will give you a good time." And he winked.
So Arnie asked me out.

It just so happened I saw Arnie playing basketball
with my

brother, so I said yes. I didn't realize Arnie was the
same guy

that took one friend out on Friday night and the other
friend

out on Saturday night. We came to Sheepshead Bay. I was
dressed up, not knowing we were going on a rowboat. I
said

to myself, "Never again. What a cheapskate." After a few
minutes he said, "Do you see that yacht over there? Do you
like it?" I said yes. He said, "That belongs to my father." And
that's where we ended up. The other couple disappeared to
a state room. We sat on the deck in the moonlight talking.
Of course he put his arm around me and tried to kiss me. I
thought, "Some nerve. I hardly know him." And that
was that.

About a month later I was walking with a girlfriend
at a carnival in town. I saw Arnie and Dickie and they
said hello. I wouldn't even say hello. Arnie said to Dickie,
"She seems like such a nice girl. I don't understand why
she doesn't like me." Dickie said, "I really didn't tell you
the truth about her. She *is* a nice girl." A while later Arnie
asked me out again. He said, "There is a play at the high
school a block from your house. We'll walk both ways."

I finally said yes.

DOUBLE DATE

We went out for months and really liked
each other. He opened the car door for me

and acted like a real gentleman. I was his
only date, Friday and Saturday. He had
a problem. His mother didn't like the fact
that he was going steady at nineteen. She
insisted he take out one of her friends' daughters.
I said, "What am I supposed to do Saturday night?"
We were both unhappy until I came up with a
bright idea. I would a get a date and we could go
out, two couples. I called a tall handsome guy who
I knew who lived in New York and asked him to take
me out.

So the four of us went out. I was watching
this girl snuggle up to Arnie in the front seat. I
didn't like it. Arnie was also unhappy, seeing my
date kiss my cheek in the back seat. We went to Carl
Hopples and ate and danced. My date didn't drive, so
when Arnie offered to drive him to the subway, he said,
No, I'm going to stay at Irene's for a while. Arnie almost
died. He went home and told his parents he loved me and
not to butt in again in no uncertain terms. The girl told
her mother, "I think Arnie loves Irene because he kept
looking at her." That was it. We were a couple.

ENGAGEMENT

We went together for a year. We had
a lot of fun. Arnie belonged to a fraternity
at NYU and they had one party after another.
Arnie joined the Army with the ROTC. Because

he volunteered driving an ambulance for Mary
Immaculate Hospital, he wanted to go into
the medical corps. But they put him in the Army
Air Corps. I went to visit him twice with his mom.
We had a wonderful relationship. She loved me
like a daughter. One of our trips to see him was
to Colorado. And one was to Kansas City. Then
he went overseas. He was shipped to Calcutta
India as an aerial photographer. He sent many
pictures home of India and the people there.
It was three years before he came back. During
that time I spent many hours with his family. We
wrote to each other every day. When he came back
it was to Fort Dix. We were very excited. His mother
and I had made plans for our wedding. Almost
immediately I said, "Arnie, we are getting married in
nine days." He didn't say anything immediately. He was
in shock. It was at the Essex House in New York. We
had thirty people, the immediate family. It cost my
father $500, which was a lot in those days. Then I was
a married lady. I was twenty-one.

INTERFAITH

My grandparents were very religious, but
my father was not religious because of eight
years in the American Army. All the same, my
father insisted because I was the oldest that I only go
out with Jewish boys. I was the only one of his

children who married a Jewish person.
My brother Lou and his girlfriend Ruth eloped.
My parents were upset until they met Ruth. My brother
Charlie met an English girl at work. They married.
My sister Marion married a non-Jewish man. Two of
my four children intermarried. They were all happily
married. My son Richard married a beautiful girl
from Equador, Fiorella. She is the nicest person I
ever met. They all turned out well. I believe that
if people fall in love, it doesn't matter what faith
the other person is. This is today's world.

MY ADVENTURES

MY FIRST ROMANCE
1940

I was sixteen. My parents allowed
me to go to a dance at the Creswin
Hotel. They wouldn't allow me to
go to Manhattan to a dance, but my
mother's four brothers were running
a dance at the Creswin every Saturday
night and they promised my mother
they would take care of me. I took four
girlfriends with me. I bought a black
dress and wore a white flower in my
hair.

The bandleader was very handsome.
He looked like Gene Raymond, the actor.
He kept looking at me. And finally he
asked me to dance.

I fell in love immediately.

He had to take a train and a bus to Queens
to visit me.

We went together for a year.

One day he suggested I should meet him
in Manhattan and go up to the Bronx
to see how far he had to travel just to see me.

I was very naive.

In his apartment he took my coat off,
picked me up and threw me on the bed.

I punched him. He fell off the bed.

He took me home and never called again.

UP AND DOWN

I decided to visit my fiancee in Salina, Kansas.
I asked my boss for two weeks' vacation and he gave
it to me. I stayed with my fiancee's partner Bert and his
wife
Olga, who were also in Salina, Kansas. It took the train
three
days to get there. It was filled with Army men. When
the train
stopped in Chicago, a sailor got on. He sat in the empty
seat
next to me. He was so tired he fell asleep and his head
dropped on my shoulder. I didn't wake him. He slept for
one whole hour. One of the soldiers called me a traitor.

In Salina Arnie and Bert were in the same Army base
and Olga also worked there. I decided to get a job because
I was alone all day. I found a job as an elevator operator.
The hotel management show me how to push this big
wheel from floor to floor. The name of the hotel was The
Warren. It was just for officers. There were seven floors. I
was eighteen and pretty so every time a soldier got on he
would say, "How about coming to my room?" It was fun
and I made nineteen dollars

a week.

Arnie and I had a wonderful time together, but all of
a sudden Arnie said, "I'm leaving in the morning."

He left. I left. And I didn't see him for three years.
He was sent to Calcutta, India as an aerial photographer.

WHO WAS KENNY RUTH
1942

In my synagogue in Saint Albans
we had a new program. The young
ladies were going to Saint Albans
Naval Hospital to entertain the sailors.
and serve them tea and cookies. I heard
some of the sailors say, "I'd rather be at the
corner bar."

One young sailor approached and spoke
to me. He was lonely, he said, and far from his home
in Ohio. When he told me his name, Kenny Ruth,
I asked if he were any relative to Babe Ruth.
The answer was no.

My mother loved to cook for service men, so
I asked him to walk over to my house for dinner. I lived
three blocks away. He came to dinner and enjoyed
playing cards with my sisters and brothers and me.
He started to come over every week. My family
looked forward to his visits. About a year later
Kenny called me and asked me to buy him a carton
of cigarettes and to meet him about six o'clock

in front of the gate. And I did. He wasn't there.

I went over to the guard. who looked at the list
and said, "There is no Kenny Ruth registered here."

ADVICE

I had a wonderful mother-in-law.
The first time I came to her house,
she was on the phone. She was chairperson
of the cheer committee of the temple.
I never heard of this before, helping people
cheering them up. When I got married,
she advised me to join the temple, join
B'nai Brith and join Hadassah. I listened
to her and it helped me to have a very happy
full life, helping people and making many many
friends. Eventually I became president of five
big organizations, Temple Sisterhood, President
of a B'nai Brith Chapter, President of B'nai Brith
Council, and President of Cinema Radio TV unit
of B'nai Brith, and President of Jewish Women
International here in Long Beach.

COUNTRY LIFE
1947

Many years ago my in-laws had a couple
working for them, a housekeeper and a
gardener. I thought they were very old

but they were only in their sixties.
They decided to retire in New Hampshire.
When my husband and I took a trip through
New England, we decided to visit the Bakers.
They had a farmhouse and a farm and seemed
very happy. I couldn't sleep too well because
they had baby chickens in the next room and the
odor was horrible.

The next morning we looked forward to a
country breakfast, pancakes, bacon, etc. I'll
never forget our disappointment. We were
served white bread and a cold hard-boiled
egg.
Next stop: a diner.

MY FRIEND PEARL, OH WHAT A GIRL

I was at a meeting in 1948 at my temple
in Elmont. I said to my friend Alice Kramer,
Who is arguing with the speaker. The lady was
arguing with the speaker. Alice said, "That
is Pearl Blank."

A while later the temple had a show. I went
into the dance group. We danced to "Five foot
two / eyes of blue / Could she, could she / could she
coo." And who was in the same group but Pearl
Blank.

My husband did the scenery and met Pearl's
husband Jerry. They became fishing friends.

So Pearl and I got friendlier. She had beautiful
blue eyes and a terrific sense of humor. Her
husband owned Paragon Sporting Goods, one
of the biggest sporting goods companies in the
world. We were lucky. Our husbands could afford
to send us to Florida for a month. At that time we
each had two kids and I brought my housekeeper
Mary along, who prayed all the way to Florida.
The men came down and spent one week with us
and one week in Green Turtle Cay to go deep sea
fishing. One night Pearl and I walked on the promenade
to visit Pearl's inlaws. The hostess introduced us to a
group of men from the Five Towns. They invited us
to go to the races the next day. Pearl said yes, I said no.
The next day as Pearl and the men drove up so did the
two husbands. Pearl got out of the car after having a
wonderful time and introduced the men to Arnie and
Jerry. That evening my husband said to me, "Why didn't
you go?" I looked at him and said, "I didn't think you'd
like me
going to the races with a bunch of men." He laughed
and said, "Why not?" I looked at him in astonishment and
suddenly I understood why I did not go.

I believed that on account of my childhood I was held
back from doing a lot of the things I wanted to do socially.
Watching Pearl I understood how it was to be free of all
these
worries. She really helped me understand how to be less
afraid
of life.

BRUCE BLANK
2013

I sit at the seder table with my old friend Pearl Blank
as her son, Bruce Blank, now sixty-two, reads aloud from the
seder text with authority and runs the proceedings, and
I look
into the past and remember my thirty-fifth birthday

    Pearl and I were going out for a short lunch, just
the two
of us, for though Bruce was home from school, he was ill
with a cold.

    Before we left, Pearl mentioned to him that it was my
birthday.

    When we came back, he was standing at the kitchen
door,
calling us to come in. He was only nine years old.

    While we were out, he had baked a cake. The table
was set,
and next to my plate was an envelope containing all the
change
he had saved up during the year, a birthday gift for me.

    He is now the president of Paragon Sporting Goods,
one of the largest sporting goods companies in the world.

THE BLUE KITCHEN

When I worked in New York I had lunch
in the Blue Kitchen almost every day. This

young fellow, a busboy, always smiled and blushed when I came in. One day I walked in and again he smiled and blushed as usual but this time he bumped into a waitress who spilled her tray, which caused a big stir. Several people rushed over, shouting at him, and cleaned up the mess. Next thing I knew he was sitting at my table. He told me he had just been fired on account of his clumsiness and I suppose I may have felt a little guilty for having distracted him. His name was Murray Aronoff, he said, and he came from The Bronx. After a while he asked me to go out with him. I said no because I was engaged and I showed him my ring. He said, "I'd like to be your friend," and I said okay.

Every day he met me as I was leaving my office. He took the train with me to Jamaica and then went home to the Bronx. He seemed very lonely so one day I said, "Tomorrow come all the way home with me and you can meet my brother and sister. Maybe you can play cards with them."

He said okay. He came every weekendand they got to be good friends. Our mother was happy to include him for dinner. Then the war ended and Arnie came home. I invited Murray and his sister to the wedding ceremony. I never saw him again until years later at a convention for B'nai Brith.

It was held in Toronto, Canada. The programfeatured Leon Uris who wrote the book Exodus. There on the stage he introduced the crew of the ship The Exodus. To my surprise one was Murray Aronoff. I said to my friend

Pearl, "I know him." She said, "Go back stage and say hello," which
I did. I said, "Hello, Murray." He looked blank and didn't remember me. I said, "We met at The Blue Kitchen and then you came out to my home in St. Albans for a year." He didn't remember. Then I came back to my seat and told Pearl, "He doesn't remember me."

Pearl told the president of B'nai Brith who went to the microphone and said, "Can you imagine anyone not remembering Irene?"

Two years later I read in an obituary that Murray Aronoff at the age of fifty died of Alzheimer's Disease.

BUSINESS TRIP
1978

I was going on a business trip to California
with my partner Sam and his wife Ruth. Arnie
decided to join us. Janis, who was thirteen, was
left home with a baby sitter. She called friends
and had a party at the house. When we called
from California, the sitter said it was late and the
kids were still there. I called a friend to go over
and see that the kids went to sleep.
Arnie decided to go home as he had
been to California and he wanted to make sure
that Janis was okay.

I continued on the trip. We made a few
stops with motion picture companies

to increase our business. Then as planned we went
to San Diego to see Sam's brother. There wasn't
enough room for me to stay so they drove me to
a motel in the area. I was there for a few minutes
and the phone rang and someone said, "I see you
are in your room alone." I was scared and piled
all the furniture against the door. I could not sleep
and stayed up all night. The next morning I went
to the coffee shop in the motel. A man who was in
the Navy years before and knew everyone started
to talk to me. He said, "Young lady, have you ever
been to Mexico?" I said no. And he said he would
gladly show me around. Of course I never planned
to go. When Sam and his brother came to take me
to the airport I kidded them and said, "I was going
to go to Mexico with this man." They each took one
arm and practically carried me to the airport.

HOW I GOT INTO MOTION PICTURES

As I was president of the Freeport chapter
of B'nai Brith Women, I went to a convention
at the Concord Hotel. Our group had fourteen people.

One night when I was walking down the
marble hall I saw a man and looked at his badge.
It said Sam Silverstein. I said to him, "I know
a Sam Silverstein, but you are not him. He is a client
of my husband and he comes from Pittsburgh."

Sam said, "I grew up in Pittsburgh."

We started to talk. He was president of the B'nai

Brith lodge in Inwood, Manhattan.

I said, "Oh, there's an Inwood near me. But it's not the same one."

He looked at my badge that said "Freeport" and asked where that was.

I told him, then mentioned how elderly his group was. They were in wheelchairs and used crutches and he was vigorous and young, about fifty. So I said to him, "My group Nassau
Suffolk Council is having a big dance tonight. Why don't you come. You would enjoy it. There are people your age."

I was surprised when he walked in. I did know he worked
for a motion picture company. I also knew that Seymore who was president of the Freeport Lodge was an accountant who bought motion pictures for his clients as tax shelters. The two men were a perfect match, so I introduced them. Before the night was over they decided to start a new company, and they asked me to be the third partner without having to put money in. And I accepted.

MY VACATION IN ISRAEL
2007

Some times I sit and wander
through the photos of us all.
Memories buried within my mind
like prayers in the Western Wall.
But the clarity is wearing thin

and the past feels like a maze.
I recall feeling like I was part
of the Bible back in the olden days.
A tour guide who was once a captain
in the Israeli army brought us to the sights.
And the land left us in awe.
Although I must admit I shook with fright
atop a camel with a giant paw.
Looking at the endless steps of Masada
caused my joints to shake and my eyes to tear,
but the kids and I united at the zealots' last frontier.
They took the challenge while I opted for the tram,
and together we saw ruins
we could never find in the states of Uncle Sam.
If you would like to go under a spell
on your next vacation go to Israel.

Written By: Mariel Falk

THE PLEDGE

The Fourth of July when I was a little girl
I loved when we had to sing *The Star Spangled
Banner*. It made me feel so patriotic. I loved
my country and would never think of living
in another country. At one time the town of
Hempstead had fireworks that were exciting.
Friday night the thirteenth they were having
fireworks in Long Beach. I wondered why Friday night.
Well, the next two days were a craft fair. And

this helped advertise the fair. I remember last
year people on the boardwalk shoulder to
shoulder staring up in wonder at the beautiful
fireworks. On the beach were whole families
having picnics.

At some of our meetings I notice when *The
Pledge Of Allegiance* is announced, some people
stand up and put their hands on their hearts.
Then they sing *The Star Spangled Banner.* Some
people talk and walk around and pay no attention. Maybe
some of the seniors are hard of hearing.

TODAY
July 23, 2013

I had an appointment at ten-thirty with
the skin doctor for my yearly check-up. I
took the power bus and told the driver Keon
to pick me up at eleven-thirty. The office was
very crowded and I wasn't called by eleven-thirty.
I told Dawn the receptionist I would come back
on a rainy day when I had nothing to do.

The bus took me back to JASA where I did
exercise with my favorite person Lisa. She plays
music. Her smile is contagious. We do the mambo
senior style. We then had a delicious lunch and socialized.

By the time I came home and answered my phone
messages it was three o'clock. Even though I loved
swimming I was too lazy to put my bathing suit on. I

decided to go down to the pool deck and sit at a table in the shade and write.

So here I am.

I keep thinking how lucky I am to be sitting in this beautiful place and resting. My cell phone rang and it was my friend Renee. She invited me to come home to her place after JASA tomorrow, bring my bathing suit, swim in her pool and then have dinner. She said, "I will not take no for an answer." And I said, "Yes, I will come."

And then she said there is a party in her building on Saturday. All of her family is coming and she wants me to meet them. I said I would come.

It's unusual for me to sit and not run around. But I'm enjoying it.

TEXTING

I visited my daughter Janis in Florida
during the storm Sandy. My three granddaughters
Samantha, 12, Jessica, 10, and Juliet, 8, were
texting all the time. They asked me if I knew how
to text. I said no. They couldn't believe their
grandmother didn't know how to text. They showed
me. I didn't understand. So Samantha wrote down
instructions for me. When I got home, they texted
me. I didn't text back. I called them. I said it's too much
trouble. I couldn't see the letters on my cell phone
without putting on my glasses and using a magnifying
glass. I told them I would call them on the phone instead.

129

MY GRANDPA NATHAN

He was a cheerful man with sparkling blue eyes.
He used to visit us in Laurelton from Brooklyn.
The minute he walked in he cheered everyone up.
He always asked me (I was the oldest) to play cards,
but I don't remember the name of the game. One time
he came to visit and had some trouble. All the houses
in Laurelton looked the same. Tinted stucco. Peach, pink
and yellow, etc. He walked into the wrong house. The man
who was shaving chased him with a razor. Grandpa never
ran so fast in his life. He finally found our house.

MY YOUNGEST BROTHER

Jackie always bragged about looking
very young and having a nice sun tan.
He never married and lived alone, but he
seemed happy with his life. He called
me every night at eleven.

He would always begin by saying, "What's
going on?"

And then we would talk.

One night he called me and said.
"I was just in an accident. They took my car,
stole my wallet."

I begged him to go to the hospital.

For a day or two I couldn't get him to answer
the phone.

So I called the Jewish Family Service in
Houston, Texas. They found him in a hospital.
He had no identification. The hospital knew
nothing about him.

We never found out what really happened, but
we speculated that he'd had a stroke, because
he had a severe case of diabetes. He
suffered another six months and passed away
on December 28, 2010, at the age of sixty-seven.
I had the body brought to Long Island
to be buried in the family plot in Pinelawn Cemetery
in Farmingdale. My brother Charlie had traveled twice
from
California to Texas to visit Jackie before the end, but fell
ill just before the funeral and was unable to be there.

I attended accompanied only by my friend Arline.

DEFAMATION

I'm not anti-Semitic, but my dog is.
I tried to find out why he was so prejudiced.
One thing I knew about him is it was very
obvious he was not circumcised. I found out
he was born a Roman Catholic and was baptized and
was told never to associate with anyone who was Jewish.
When
I adopted him, he almost plotzed. Not only would
he not associate with Jewish humans, he wouldn't
associate with Jewish dogs. When they barked, it wasn't

the way he barked. He would bark woof like any good
Catholic dog. They would bark Oy woof already yet.
Then one day he met Hannah Naomi Cohen, a Jewish
poodle. They fell in love. They got married in a secret
ceremony, conducted by a Rabbi Rottweiler, but her
family
found out and crashed the wedding. You never saw so
many
dogs wearing yarmulkes in your life. Hannah Naomi's
mother
was running around barking, "But he is not Jewish!"
Once
the couple were married, they didn't keep kosher, but lived
happily ever after.

by Irene Levy and Charles Rubin

LAUGHTER

Mama

I now feel guilty. I wasn't that nice
to my mother. I didn't understand.
Now I do.

One day I went to the movies
with her. She loved Laurel and Hardy.
She had a loud hearty laugh. She laughed
so loud I was embarrassed. I said, "Mama,

why are you laughing so loud?"

In her last years I wished she could laugh.
I would give anything to hear her laugh again.

Daddy

Even at the end Daddy made me laugh.
He was in the hospital in New York, very
ill. I picked up my mother and drove her
to New York, with Janis in the car, only
three years old. It was very hard for me.
Finally one day I showed her how to take
a taxi and a train to New York. She
started to do it by herself. Even though
my father was very ill he joked around.
He spoke Spanish to the porters, but it was a fake
Spanish that he made up, a nonsense language
that sounded like Spanish, and it always got
the porters and everyone else laughing.
He died with a smile on his face.

* * *

AFTERWORD

Arnie and I had four wonderful children. Andrea Levy married Kenneth Smith and they live in Atlanta GA. They have two sons: Jeffrey and Daniel. Daniel is married to Ana Carla and has a baby girl named Sidonia. Richard Levy married Fiorella. They have two sons, Andrew and Alex, and live in Atlanta, GA.

Linda Falk lives in Mamaroneck, New York and has two daughters: Mariel and Aliya. Janis Rosenberg lives in Jensen Beach, Florida and has three daughters: Samantha, Jessica and Juliette.

I am now ninety-one years old and living in Long Beach.

I moved here sixteen years ago after my wonderful husband, Arnold, passed away. My friend, Audrey Gelzer, lived here as well. I moved into her building at 420 Shore Road, but there was no parking space. Two years later, my daughter Linda bought me a two-bedroom apartment at 522 Shore Road, with parking, facing the ocean. I absolutely I love it.

I go to Temple Emmanuel just about every Sabbath. I stopped driving, but a bus picks me up every day and takes me to JASA, a senior-citizen group. There, I participate in wonderful programs, exercise, and get a nice lunch for just three dollars. I also go to Jewish Women International, which used to be B'nai Brith Women. I am on three boards, have many friends, and simply love it here.

Printed in the United States
By Bookmasters